# THE PERFORMANCE PAPERS

# THE
# PERFORMANCE PAPERS

## ANDREW BASS

First Published in Great Britain 2011 by Bookshaker

© Copyright Andrew Bass PhD

# CONTENTS

**Contents**
**Acknowledgments**
**Foreword by Jens R. Höhnel**

# ACKNOWLEDGMENTS

Many colleagues and clients have contributed both directly and indirectly to the development of *The Performance Papers* – some of whom must remain nameless for reasons of commercial confidentiality (you know who you are, and I thank you). I am very pleased to be able to acknowledge the insight, inspiration and top-quality critique I have received from Jens Höhnel, Alan Weiss, John Handley Alastair Dryburgh, Helga Henry, Barbara Clarke, Karl Pestell, Jules Hancox, Peter Selkirk, Richard Goodier, Cora Lynn Heimer Rathbone, Charlie Wilson, Lucy McCarraher, Joe Gregory and Stephen Bass.

# FOREWORD

This book will be of great benefit to anyone who wants to develop their people, organization and business to world class standards. It will help you to understand the interdependence between culture and strategy, leadership and people; through reading it you will gain a clear perspective on how to create a high performance organization.

Andy Bass has many years of business experience in a range of areas, in addition to which he has an impressive understanding of how to teach, train and motivate people.

This book lays out the importance of culture as "the beliefs and values that influence behaviour" in an organization. It also confirms my own experience that executing a business strategy depends, in the end, on people's performance and behaviour. It demonstrates very clearly that real success results from pursuing two interrelated paths: the business goals *and* the behaviour of people.

My personal experience, being a CEO in the extremely competitive environment of automotive suppliers, is that we need a better understanding of how *all* the elements of our businesses are tied together. That way we grasp what makes us more competitive and successful in our global markets.

To effectively develop, produce and market new products requires target-oriented, interdisciplinary teamwork among all the areas involved in each specific customer project, for instance in my own business this would include Engineering and Design, Manufacturing, Controlling, Purchasing, Finance, Marketing and Sales. In other words, it requires a high performance organization.

IAC (International Automotive Components Group) has integrated six acquisitions over the last four years and you can imagine how important it is for such a business structure to establish a common company culture – not just on paper, but lived and loved. Acquisitions always bring new employees with specific behaviours, developed over years. Once you have bought a new company you will definitely have their "bodies", but what you need is their "brain" and, even more, you want their "heart". Once you have achieved that, you will have motivated people. And these people will be able to achieve also your business goals.

Looking at demographic developments over the next five to ten years we are going to be faced with a lack of young, well-educated and business-minded people. For any company with the need for qualified employees, it will be key to develop and train their next generation leaders. These "emerging leaders" and high potentials will be crucial for a successful future and will be essential in growing a business. HR managers and management are not only challenged to find the right people but also to retain and motivate the next generation of leadership.

Our next generation leaders at IAC have attended a Leadership Development Programme at the Aston Business School Centre for Executive Development which was outstanding and highly valued by all participants.

The IAC people are also benefitting hugely from the content of this book and additionally from Andy's exceptional expert guidance for aligning our people with our objectives and turning strategy into action.

You can read this book without getting disoriented by arcane jargon or "sophisticated" terminology. It is exactly what you want and need to know – based on solid business background and real life experience. This book is relevant and advantageous for everyone who wants to create a high performance organization.

**Jens R. Höhnel**
**CEO / President Europe**
**International Automotive Components Group (IAC)**

# INTRODUCTION

As a consultant to leaders, my concern is simple: to help them to improve performance, both of individuals and their organizations as a whole. I do this in a variety of ways: from one-to-one coaching, through organizational consulting, facilitation of strategy and group decision making, speaking keynotes and workshops, and in the current way: by writing.

My clients are competent and committed people. So why do they seek help?

- The day to day demands of the job almost inevitably block their access to their ideas, skills, competences and resources because they are so close to things. It's not always the "unknown unknowns" that are the problem, it's the "unknown knowns" – those things that could solve your problem if only you could step back long enough to perceive them, probably from a new angle.

- Not all their colleagues share either their competence or commitment. No need to be too diplomatic here – Sartre said that "Hell is other people" – a bleak view (sometimes heaven is other people too!) but I am sure that all readers who have been in business for a while can think of examples of people without whom things would go much more smoothly.

- They haven't always got people they can rely on as sounding boards or amplifiers of their own thinking (when you are the leader, you can't always involve your people in your early thoughts because they find it almost impossible not to filter their advice through their instantaneous calculation of the impact on their own futures).

- "Order tends to chaos." Busy leaders need help in reordering things and recreating the simplicity that supports effective decisions and action.

In this book I've collected together and re-edited a set of the papers and articles I have written for clients (increasingly with their incisive feedback during the writing process – something I have always be grateful for and which has led to more learning for both them and me in the process).

Because I work with general managers (and those who aspire to be), the chapters span a wide variety of topics – strategy, growth, leadership, organization and organizational change, executive effectiveness and managing individual performance. The chapters are sequenced in a logical order if you want to read the book straight through, but they are also intended to be easy to dip into as standalone pieces. I want the book to be of practical help as well as be thought provoking, and for a busy manager that will often mean being able to turn to the relevant page and quickly get a new idea or tool.

## Guiding Themes

There are of course some guiding themes, and it will be useful to introduce them here. In my experience, these are leverage points where much improvement potential lies. I have picked out four; two outward facing ones, and two about internal organization.

### *External:*

1. Maintaining focus on value as experienced by the customer.

2. Keeping your people focused on return-on-investment – the educational task of the leader.

**Internal:**

3. Refusing to warrant "them and us" thinking – deliberately or inadvertently.

4. Constantly maintaining and improving the match-up between words and deeds.

Let's have a look at each of these in turn.

## 1. Maintaining focus on value as experienced by the customer

It is so easy to forget the simple idea that people exchange money for something they perceive as more valuable than the money. This is easiest to see in consumer markets, but it is just as true in B2B.

At one time it was a cliché to quote the great management thinker Peter Drucker, but remarkably[1], fewer people seem to be aware of him now, so I am going to go for it:

> *"The aim of marketing is to know and understand the customer so well the product or service fits him and sells itself."*

Another excellent way of thinking about it, which I first heard in a talk by Paul Fifield, is that the purpose of marketing is to enable you to get the price you want.

Both of these are pointing us in the same direction: we need to deeply understand what the person who will sign the cheque really values.

## 2. Keeping people focused on return-on-investment – the educational task of the leader

Oscar Wilde famously quipped that "A cynic is a man who knows the price of everything but the value of nothing". Even in happy and non-cynical companies, most employees know about cost, but remarkably few think about return.

---

[1] As my colleague Alastair Dryburgh pointed out to me recently.

What ideas do your people have about money? Most of the people who join you have little or no idea about return-on-investment (unless, perhaps, they had entrepreneurial parents) and so they typically look at the cost side of the equation and not the potential return. With tenacity, you can make a huge difference by educating them. One of the finest executives I know told me about an organization she had worked in that revolutionised performance by the simple measure of constantly reminding people to think about any money spent as an investment. It was as simple as responding to requests for money, *any* requests, with a questions such as, "What will the return be?" Pretty easy and obvious but rare indeed, especially in larger corporations (and even more especially in non-operating departments).

### 3.  Refusing to warrant 'them and us' thinking

I'm on safe ground if I suggest that leaders probably spend more time refereeing turf wars than they would like. The easy but fatal mistake for a manager is to take sides because you have been biased by the impassioned them-and-us story you got from the first party to reach your office. Here are some of the things you hear constantly in organizations:

It's corporate...
It's the X division...
It's the IT department...
It's HR...
It's finance...
It's Generation Y... (okay, this one is true)
It's compliance...
It's the customers...

It's important to rise above the fray, and a good starting point is to be deeply suspicious of 'explanations' of behaviour that assume that the person or group concerned is mad, bad or dangerous. They just may be, but it is far, far more likely that their behaviour would seem quite reasonable if you could adopt their very different standpoint.

If you are a leader, then as soon as you allow a remark which generalises about accountants, headquarters or Bob to pass without comment, you have given it your warrant – and it will become part of the reality you now have to manage. On a related note, be very careful about the use of personality tests which generalise behaviour into a few categories. And if you are a Myers-Briggs fan, don't get defensive – I am allegedly an INTP which apparently explains my scepticism about the MBTI. Similarly I am told that my disbelief in astrology stems from my being a Virgo.

## 4. Constantly maintaining and improving the match-up between words and deeds

In all industries and sectors, private, public and non-profit, I am still continually struck by the curious, but almost universal tendency of both organizations and individuals to say one thing and do another. In truth, this is not confined to organizational life – it's a basic thing that humans do everywhere.

Most organizations have similar corporate values concerning things like shareholder value, "our people", safety, teamwork and ethics, and the seriousness with which these are treated are flatly contradicted by observable behaviour as reported in the business press daily:

- If shareholder value were the overriding consideration, the plush offices, perks, jets and country club memberships (and – to be more controversial – a good deal of the corporate social responsibility and cultural sponsorship activity) would not exist.

- If people were the greatest resource, then loyal middle managers with invaluable tacit knowledge of your business would be some of the last, rather than first, people to be made redundant in downturns.

- If safety were the top priority, everyone from oil companies to railway operators would reward employees for stopping unsafe operations rather than pressuring them to defy the laws of physics.

- If it was really a management *team*, then departmental or divisional heads would share resources, and not resist reallocation of funds to their most profitable uses.

- If ethics were so important, salespeople and traders with good numbers but sharp practices would be moving out rather than up.

Well you get the idea.

We need less double-speak. We've all heard more than our fair share of managers using language straight out of the politician's 'media training' playbook to tell staff how much they and the company values matter. Because these managers – like the politicians they emulate – don't really have their fingers on the pulse, they actually think they are being believed when in fact they are eroding their potential control of their operations, and creating cynicism which makes organizing anything extremely hard.

The best managers don't deal in double-speak, and the best organizations have far less of this kind of behaviour than most (and, importantly, are unimpressed by it in promotion rounds).

## THE REALITY OF MANY CORPORATE GOALS

Russell Ackoff – one of the pioneers of systems thinking in business – used his keynote address at a 2004 conference at the prestigious Wharton School to tell a fascinating story about organizational decision-making. A major US-based multinational asked a consultant to do a study of corporate goals. The stated goals were the usual things I have mentioned: increase shareholder value, be a good corporate citizen, be the employer of choice etc. The typical stuff you find on any large company's website. The consultant looked at major decisions taken by key decision-makers over the previous five years of the business's history, and found that every such decision *violated* at least one of the stated goals. How could this be explained? Well, there were two possibilities – either management were stupid and incompetent, or the stated goals were not the real goals. Dilbert-loving cynics might conclude the former, but the consultant knew the organization well and knew that management were far from stupid. He reasoned that the *real* goals must be *unstated* ones. Could he work backwards and deduce what the real goals must be? In the end, he found that one goal explained over 90% of all corporate decisions: the real goal was to *improve the circumstances – working conditions, benefits, power and promotion etc. – of the decision taker!*

Ackoff found (as have I) that every executive he asked about this finding would admit, at least in private, that that's the way that things really work. This is one of those weird discoveries that is both surprising and not surprising at the same time. If executives are just following their own self-interest, how come companies succeed, which a great number obviously do? I think the answer is that they succeed depending on how aligned the decision maker's interests and those of the company's owners are.

What are the implications? A basic one is to simply work *with* human nature and align incentives accordingly: you can trust people to behave in their own perceived best interests. More on this later on.

# *How To Use This Book*

As I mentioned earlier, you can read straight through, or you can dive in according to where your current need takes you.

My aim in all my writing is to avoid unnecessary jargon, terminology and verbiage, while at the same time ensuring that the ideas are technically "right" and could be backed up in detail if required.

The chapters are broadly sequenced so as to deal with strategy, leadership, culture and teamwork. To give you a general idea of where I stand on each, here are some big picture remarks to start with:

- The truth about *strategy* is that almost everyone except consultants hates it! On the face of it that's hard to understand – surely leaders should be interested in questions about how their business makes money and will continue to do so in the future? It makes more sense, however, when we accept that answering such questions is usually a massive hassle, requiring hard thinking and often heated discussion and ultimately demanding committed action in the face of imperfect information. No wonder so many management teams prefer to get enmeshed in operational detail which they should be delegating.

- Practically speaking, *leadership* is about getting things done through other people. Given that you don't want to stand over them the whole time, you have to figure out how to tap into people's intrinsic *self*-motivation. Often that is a matter of how you communicate your goals, and how you educate and explain the business and the things happening in the world around it. You'll need to join the dots up for people so that they come to understand how their best interests and yours can be aligned.

- There's a verb hiding inside the word *culture*: "cultivate". Just like cultivating a garden, creating a culture to support high performance is an ongoing process which never ends. I'd argue that anyone who has difficulty accepting that fact is going to have a hard time leading an organization. Values such as collaboration and teamwork don't just happen because you put nice posters on the wall – their cultivation is a never-ending, full-contact activity.

- Many so-called *teams* are actually no such thing. A real team plays together as a coordinated entity, with the aim of triumphing over external competitors or circumstances – *not* over each other – and with the expectation that they will *share* the rewards of success, or the penalties of failure. Let's face it, many actual workgroups are beset with internal competition for resources and credit. You can argue that this is inevitable, and in some circumstances can actually be useful as a spur to performance. Maybe so. What is corrosive is having people pretend to work together when they are not doing so: that just creates a hall of mirrors in which agreements don't stick and there's a frustrating lack of follow-through, often without apparent explanation. Rather than keeping up appea-rances, it's much better – and releases all kinds of energy – for workgroups to acknowledge and accom-modate conflicting interests.

*Introduction*

In addition to the main text, you'll find sidebars within the chapters. The saying goes that there is nothing so useful as a good theory. That's true, as long as you act on the theory. So if you are in a hurry, these sections are for you. The articles in the sidebars first appeared in my online newsletter (subscribe at *www.bassclusker.com*). Each sidebar stands alone and is designed to be read in less than four minutes. Sometimes, as a busy manager, that might be all the time you have to get a new idea you can use to challenge you and your organization to think and act differently.

With that, let's dive in.

# CHAPTER ONE

# THE THREE COMPELLING BUSINESS STORIES YOU MUST TELL AND ANIMATE

Any business leader has got to be able to articulate three compelling stories, and then be able to turn those three stories into reality. The stories are:

- The customer (or client) story – which vividly portrays your promise to those people who will provide you with revenue.

- The talent story – which mobilises the commitment of the people who will enable you to make good on your promise.

- The investment story – which attracts and convinces those people who will provide the backing for your business (in whatever form or mixture, whether from a boss, a corporate centre or external investor) and want to understand their likely return.

It's amazing how much mental clutter you can clear if you think about your endeavour in these terms.

Figure 1.1 shows that you are competing in three markets at the same time – and suggests that you need to position yourself in the sweet spot where you have compelling stories for each of those markets simultaneously.

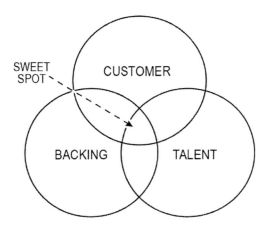

Figure 1.1: The three compelling stories you need about your endeavour

Here are some examples of compelling stories told by well-known companies:

- **Customer Stories:** FedEx for many years used to make the simple, compelling customer promise "when it absolutely has to be there overnight". When Apple trailed the latest iPhone they produced an internet video in which Apple developers discussed their enthusiasm for the products as users themselves. One designer talked about how he could use the video phone to talk to his kids at college. He said the iPhone enabled him to "look into their eyes and see how they were *really* doing". There is no comparison between that customer story and the usual tallying-up of megapixels and gigabytes.

- **Talent Stories:** The John Lewis Partnership offers recruits the opportunity to be partners in leading UK retail businesses Waitrose and John Lewis, in which the profits, benefits and pride resulting from success will be shared with them. Tesco offers a graduate training programme which students compete fiercely to enter; they know that having it on their CV will give them a long-lived asset of high value.

- **Investor Stories:** An obvious example is Berkshire Hathaway. Warren Buffett is the world's most famous investor, and has made many of his investors rich. His annual letters to stockholders explain and educate his strategy and philosophy and combine with his track record to lead many people to aspire to Berkshire ownership.

Further examples abound: the daily business press is filled with instances of managers seeking funds from investors who are more or less sceptical about the proposition.

Sometimes the decisions made by customers, talent or backers are going to be a matter of the pure numbers – technical specs, salaries, projected earnings for example – but I suspect that more often than they will admit it, people rationalise the numbers to fit what their gut tells them they want to do (for example: given the number of assumptions involved in even the most sophisticated equity valuations, it's bound to happens sometimes, isn't it?).

And what influences the 'gut'? Stories.

## *Backing Up The Three Stories*

Notice that each of the successful examples above doesn't just make and deliver a promise to one of its three audiences. If you are going to operate in the sweet spot, all three stories have to be good, and they all back each other up:

- If you visit the website of Berkshire Hathaway (an instructive thing to do for any business person), you find that Warren Buffett's welcome message is not directed to readers as investors, but as customers – you may or may not hold Berkshire stock, but first he'd like to sell you something (e.g. GEICO insurance products and Borsheims jewellery). He does the same thing at the Berkshire AGM, where each of the Berkshire's businesses set up stalls to sell products and services to stockholders. Buffet tells great customer stories and whenever I've seen interviews with people who work for him, the mentoring they get (talent story) is a big part of the attraction of working for him.

- John Lewis has to run great shops, selling products people want at good prices with excellent service, in order to make and deliver on the unique promise it offers its employees.

- And FedEx could never have funded its huge investments in surface and air transport fleets, distribution centres and logistics systems without offering investors a competitive ROI. Neither could it have created that great fund of heroic stories about getting the package through whatever it takes without making it a company people wanted to be part of – think of all those celebrated heroic tales of the lengths FedEx people went to get a package through. Similarly, Tesco's offer to the talent market is only part of the story. Its strategic mix of sophisticated logistics, data mining, working capital management etc. add up to a powerful proposition for investors. And its customer story has captured the minds and the wallets of 30% of the grocery market in the UK alone.

## Balancing The Stories

It's the leader's job to articulate these stories. It's also their job to keep them in balance. The tendency of many businesses is to favour only one or two of the promises (in particular, public company managements are often most concerned with telling stories to investors); only the best leaders keep all three balls in the air.

## What if you are out of balance?

There's a story about two colleagues from a large IT company – a salesman and a system engineer – who go hunting in the woods. Once they get to their cabin, the salesman says to the system engineer: "You make a fire, and I'll go and catch us something to eat." "OK," says the engineer happily and the salesman disappears into the forest. About an hour later the engineer is boiling some water over the fire when he hears loud screams from the trees: "Open the door! Open the door!" The salesman appears, pursued by a large and very fierce grizzly bear. The salesman rushes towards the cabin door and at the last second dodges to the side. The bear overshoots and falls through the door, which the salesman slams behind it and bolts quickly. "Phew," says the salesman, "that was close! Anyway," he says, turning to the engineer, "I've caught it, now you skin it and cook it."

## Over-relying on the customer story

There is a strong tendency among salespeople to over-egg the proposition: if you are good at selling it is quite easy to get potential customers excited about something you can't deliver, or, equally threatening, can't deliver at a profit.

Growing businesses can easily fall into this trap. People Express, the original low-cost airline, was the first to offer a service to US travellers that was more like a bus than a traditional full-service carrier. Originally it had a neat fleet of 737s, well-trained staff etc. but it grew far more quickly than it anticipated and, not wanting to turn down business, had to rapidly expand its fleet and staff, which it did by acquisition. But now it couldn't deliver the proposition to the required basic but consistent level. Its reputation rose and fell like a firework, and it went quickly out of business, having created an industry that other, better-prepared entrants (such as Southwest) quickly exploited.

Professional service firms, too, have to watch the tendency to be hypnotised by revenue. As David Maister once said, the problem professionals often have is that "they never met a billable hour they didn't like". But a billable hour is not the same as a profitable hour, or even a *billed* hour.

## Over-relying on the talent story

Investment banks have certainly been seduced by the idea that some people are disproportionately talented at trading and therefore deserve disproportionate rewards. The remuneration committees of many public companies have been similarly-minded in their negotiation of CEO contracts. These traders and CEOs have responded by offering their employers clever, one-way bets that certainly demonstrate their talent for transferring shareholder wealth to their own pockets.

At the other end of the scale, graduate recruiters share the tendency of salespeople to over-promise. This is a great way to sow the seeds of poor morale and high attrition.

## Over-relying on the investor story

This is a particular danger for public companies. There are all kinds of ways to increase perceived shareholder value in the short term which act against the real long term value. The most extreme examples are illegal, of course, think Enron and Bernie Madoff, but weren't they just taking a certain sort of more widely accepted attitude to its logical conclusion?

Consider the frenzied hype during the dotcom era where businesses with no profits (and unclear methods of ever making one) were selling for gigantic multiples of revenue. Buffett wrote a great, and remarkably-timed, shareholder letter about incomprehensible EBITDA multiples in 2000 saying, "References to Ebitda make us shudder." It's on the Berkshire Hathaway website and makes entertaining reading.

## Don't maximise one – balance three

As Figure 1.1 above makes clear, hitting the sweet spot is not about maximising one dimension, but balancing all three. Let's look at Jack Welch, *Fortune Magazine*'s Manager of the (20th) Century, when he was at GE. First of all, here's some evidence of his attention to the customer story. His schedule was available for staff to see. One GE staffer said that where the CEO in his previous company had a diary that looked like this:

8.00 am. Breakfast – project meeting
10.00 am. Project meeting
11.00 am. Staff meeting
1.00 pm. Lunch
2.00 pm. Project meeting
Etc.

Welch's schedule usually looked more like this:

8.00 am. Customer breakfast
10.00 am. Customer meeting
11.00 am. Analyst meeting
1.00 pm. Customer lunch

You get the idea. Welch is a controversial figure, but even if he's not your cup of tea, there's a great lesson here. Whether talking to customers, selling GE stock to Wall Street, or teaching his business philosophy and building managerial strength at GE's Crotonville, Jack Welch was always telling compelling stories.

What about you and your business?

## The Stories and Your Business (or Department)

Before we go any further, think about your answers to the following questions. Whatever kind of business you run, whatever size, and at whatever stage of maturity, your ability to answer them succinctly could unlock a lot of value and give you a huge renewal of energy and commitment.

Let's break the process down into a few stages to get the most out the exercise. Make sure you involve other members of your team – I've never seen an exercise with more ability to create a focused sense of shared business purpose (though you may argue a lot before you get there!).

1. Who are your audiences for the three stories?

2. Which customers/segments?

3. Which potential employees?

4. Which backers (corporate or external)?

5. What will move them to action?

6. How will your customer's life be better by giving you their business? Why will they chose your offer over alternative uses of their money?

7. Why would anyone want to work for you? Why will they chose to further their careers with you rather than somewhere else?

8. Why should an investor trust you with their hard-earned capital? Why should your manager allow you the budget?

9. What kind of demonstrations will be the most persuasive?

10. To your customers?

11. To your prospective colleagues?

18

12. To prospective backers?

13. Are the three stories compatible?

14. How do you hold the balance as time and circumstances change?

15. What balances are possible and economic and viable for you specifically?

Many managers tell me that they want their people to 'take more ownership' of their work, their projects, their roles and their teams. You can apply this questioning framework to coach emerging leaders at any level within an organization. It's a great way of getting people to think and act strategically.

You can also think of your own career in the same terms, whether you are an executive, entrepreneur, professional or individual contributor (for example even someone just starting out can benefit by thinking this way: their backers might include their family as well as their managers, their access to talent will include co-workers with whom they need to build relationships, and their customer might simply be their direct line manager or members of another department).

## Final Thoughts

The three stories framework gives an illuminating big picture view of a key leadership task, and it can be applied by leaders at all levels.

Since most, if not all, leaders come from one specialist background or another, they can tend to favour one of the three markets over the others: the framework and its attendant questions provide a clear and simple reminder that a general manager needs to balance all three.

It's worth noticing that The three stories framework doesn't constrain you as to the sort of story you tell: you can and will probably need to include traditional 'business case' elements, but make sure too that there is an emotional appeal: make it clear how the customer, the employee or the backer is better off *in terms of their concrete 'lived' experience* as a result of buying-in.

You will also have to ensure that you actually deliver, of course, so let's turn our attention to that in more detail.

CHAPTER TWO

# DELIVERING ON
# THE THREE STORIES

Of course, just being able to tell the three compelling stories I introduce in Chapter One is far from enough for success in business leadership: in fact, nothing creates disappointment and stubborn resentment like persuasive overselling!

The three stories have to be credible because they really are going to happen – you will have to have demonstrable ability to deliver. Usually, that will come from your ability to show that you have done something at least somewhat similar before. Table 2.1 provides a way for thinking through the balance of your stories, both in terms of persuasiveness and delivery capability.

| | | Customer | Talent | Backers |
|---|---|---|---|---|
| **Persuasiveness?** *Offers a compelling story or promise* | | A persuasive story provides the ability to sell your products and services at volumes, frequencies, prices and terms sufficient to meet your financial objectives. | A persuasive story provides the ability to attract, retain and motivate people who can help you make good on your promises to customers and backers. | A persuasive story provides the ability to attract funding required at a cost where you can offer a return. |
| **Delivery?** *Makes good on the promise, brings the story into reality* | | Delivery provides the ability to retain customers, benefit from reduced costs of acquisition (through repeat and referral business), build brand, get high quality information about what will sell in the future, avoid costs associated with failure to deliver. | Delivery creates loyalty, commitment, "ownership" type behaviour, retains knowledge, reduces unnecessary attrition costs. | Delivery provides the ability to secure ongoing funding, retain managerial control. |

Table 2.1: Persuasiveness and Delivery Capability

The three business stories (and your ability to implement them) don't just come out of thin air – you will have to test and refine them to get them right, and if you want to stay in business for any length of time, revisit and refresh them as customer, talent and financial markets evolve.

## Some Possible Configurations

Obviously, the goal – and remember it's a moving target – is the following configuration:

|  | Customers | Talent | Backers |
|---|:---:|:---:|:---:|
| Persuades? | ✓ | ✓ | ✓ |
| Delivers to? | ✓ | ✓ | ✓ |

At least until the recent blip partly caused by Terry Leahy's planned departure, an excellent example is provided by Tesco. It has managed the neat trick of appealing to all segments of its customer market, balancing the upmarket "Finest", mid-range Tesco and low-price "Value" brands, and encompassing a wide range of product categories including food, beverages, home, clothing, mobile phones and financial services. It has a similar appeal in the talent market where graduates covet places on its training scheme, and, even though in the midst of the recession, it continued its phenomenal financial performance, reporting record profits for a British retailer in the year to February 2010.

The following, less-than-ideal examples had well-publicised problems arising from a limitation in at least one box, but then recovered. This is crucial to remember before applying the diagnostic to your own business. None of these configurations need presage certain failure (unless left too late, of course).

I will cover a sample of configurations – the ones that seem to me the most frequent traps. These will be sufficient for you to get the idea and to spur your thinking and discussions about your own business. Don't just think about where you are now but – especially if you currently award yourself six ticks – think hard about where your business might be vulnerable.

## Customers love it, but it doesn't make money

This is a dangerous trap especially for earlier-stage businesses: a product or service that people love, enthusiastic staff who love providing it, but no profit. Is the enthusiasm of the customers and talent biasing you away from pulling the plug when you ought to, or perhaps it's a huge winner that just hasn't paid off yet? Clearly in this situation, serious debate and examination of the fundamental economics of the business model is needed.

|  | Customers | Talent | Backers |
|---|---|---|---|
| Persuades? | ✓ | ✓ | ? |
| Delivers to? | ✓ | ✓ | ✗ |

As many 'eyeballs' as it gets, YouTube doesn't make money, and if it weren't for Google, it would be out of business. Clearly Google still thinks it is worth the long-term bet (and I for one hope they keep it up there because it is one of the best things on the internet).

## Customers used to love it

Here's another situation where the emotional attachment of managers can create resistance to a change in direction:

| | Customers | Talent | Backers |
|---|---|---|---|
| Persuades? | ✗ | | **?**<br>have they noticed yet |
| Delivers to? | | | |

Marks & Spencer has certainly experienced this over the years (perhaps most noticeably in the late 1990s). It's easy for a successful company to lose touch with its customers and M&S for a time was too dowdy for younger buyers but too trendy for its traditional core.

## Gee, your graduate training programme sounded great, but...

Recruiters sell the intangible, and many are very persuasive. The problem is, out-sourced or staff recruiters don't have to deliver the careers they promise.

| | Customers | Talent | Backers |
|---|---|---|---|
| Persuades? | ✓ | ✓ | ✓ |
| Delivers to? | ✓ | ✗ | ✓ |

Unhappy staff tend to lead to unhappy customers and high attrition, and one of the most effective ways to create unhappy staff is to oversell them on the job. Graduate recruiters, in particular, help to create this problem by promising the earth in order to attract the best talent. Curiously, senior managers are often quite unaware of how much resentment there is among junior staff who felt they were promised more. Believe me, I and my colleagues hear this all the time in focus groups.

There's a wrinkle here: those of Generation Y can have breathtaking expectations about the nature of the work they will be doing when they join an organization. The danger is that this encourages recruiters – who are typically blissfully unaware of the trouble they are passing on to the business – to over-egg their promises even further.

If you are a large corporate or professional service firm employing relatively inexperienced but well-qualified people, I'd be amazed if this isn't going on somewhere in your operation. That might be okay in a hirer's market, but come an upturn and a lot of people will jump ship for small salary increases.

One answer is to realise that not everybody is seeking a fast-track career – in fact many people simply want a job – and to adjust your recruiting accordingly.

## *Application To Your Business*

To apply this framework to your business, extend your answers to the questions in Chapter One to include your delivery ability. Below is a blank, extended version of Table 2.1 for you to discuss with colleagues.

| | Customers | Talent | Backers |
|---|---|---|---|
| Proposition – how is this group better off with you? | | | |
| How persuasive is your story to them? *Rate (1-10)* | | | |
| How strong is your delivery ability? *Rate (1-10)* | | | |

Look for gaps and look for places where your persuasiveness and credibility could be increased. Usually the hardest thing is to become aware of the gaps; the remedies may be quite simple (although at the same time, not always easy!).

## Final Thoughts

It's probably harder to come back from poor delivery than a poor story. If your story is poor, people don't pay it much attention. If the story is good but the delivery is poor, they bring it to the attention of anyone who will listen.

You can evolve your way to a better and better story if you gain people's confidence and feedback by doing a good job on a low-value product or job, but if your actions are a let-down, they won't ever let you near something of high value to them.

---

### STATING THE (ELUSIVE) OBVIOUS

It's said that Lord Seiff, when Chairman of Marks & Spencer, would disguise himself as a tramp and visit his stores to see whether he was treated with respect. 'Undercover bosses' discover all sorts of things by going back to the shop-floor on reality TV shows. The deception may be hard or undesirable to achieve, but the fact remains that the best quality information is evident to anyone spending a few minutes to experience the business from the customer's or staff's point of view.

And it's precisely the vital information that an organization will tend to keep from its senior people, because even if you personally consider yourself approachable, many of your people have learned at one time or another that messengers get shot. Oil and banking are just two industries where we have seen risk-managers and safety-inspectors who have learned not to disturb management with inconvenient information.

---

For another example, let's go back to retailing: what is it like trying to buy consumer electricals? Here is my typical experience:

**The assistants know less than the customers**
The labels which describe alternative products only contain a few unsystematically arranged facts. But ask an assistant for the detail and all they do is read the same labels. Slower than you did, usually. Most mobile phone shops are run the same way (a notable exception in my experience is Carphone Warehouse).

**Managers banter with staff while customers stand around looking lost**
Stand in front of the group of staff looking like you need help and they don't even ignore you (that would require that they had noticed you in the first place). Request assistance, and the manager assigns the most junior of his group to you. It quickly becomes apparent that you know more about the product that they do, because at least you've had a head start reading the labels.

**They practice "anti-merchandising":
the art of making it difficult to buy**
For example: display items (on the upper shelf) don't correspond to the goods directly underneath. You see the product you want to buy on display, but then can't actually find one that's for sale! Now you have to hunt for an assistant – that means breaking into their huddle – and they will look in the same place you just did (under the display item) and then say "I don't think we've got one". Winding up customers has never been good retail practice and I don't think it's about to catch on.

Such behavioural information – unfiltered by surveys – is evident to anyone spending a few minutes experiencing their business from the customer's point of view. And it's precisely the *vital* information that an organization will tend to keep from its senior people, not just in retail, but in all sectors.

## RECOMMENDATIONS

Here's an experiment: call or visit one of your offices or departments where you will not be recognised. Don't identify yourself. If you don't like the idea of adopting a pseudonym, use your middle name. Are you treated the way you want your clients to be treated? Amazingly, in offices of higher-end service businesses, in capital city offices, and particularly with firms who consider themselves "creative" or "prestigious" (i.e. all cases where clients are worth lots of money), you may be astounded.

What's it like to deal with your business? Hiring mystery shoppers is okay but there's nothing like seeing for yourself. If you are a busy leader with position power, and are therefore vulnerable to the distorted reports of courtiers, you need ways to get your own unfiltered info. If you can, you should shop your own business, and shop the competition, too. Alan Mulally drives either a Ford or a competitor's vehicle to and from work each day. If emulating him is impossible, and there are reasons why that could be the case depending on your business, then figuring out other ways should be a priority.

CHAPTER THREE

# MANAGEMENT: IS THERE ANYTHING NEW UNDER THE SUN?

We've all heard it said that "there's nothing new under the sun" and that "everything goes back to the Greeks". And most people just nod along when they hear these clichés (although there will sometimes be someone who triumphantly points out that the Greeks didn't have laser surgery, WiFi or international jet travel).

While technological advances constantly change existing businesses and create opportunities for new ones, it's also true that the fundamentals of organizing people and resources toward productive purposes remain pretty stable over time. The builders of the pyramids clearly knew all about "execution".

Here are what I believe are four key areas that *are* changing and six areas where "the more things change, the more they stay the same".

## *What's Changing*

### Virtual teams as the new basic organizational unit

Virtual teams offer some compelling benefits, including:

- Huge savings of travel time and costs.

- The ability to get talent easily from where it is to where it's needed.

- An easy way to work with freelancers as needed (which helps to implement the appealing movie project model of organization, in which you bring together a wide variety of autonomous specialists for specific, well defined projects).

The challenges include the following:

- It's tricky to get smooth coordination and build up a shared memory.

- Communication isn't "rich"; you can't easily get nuances of voice and facial expression and it's hard to substitute for the value of those side conversations in coffee breaks that build relationships and reduce misunderstandings.

- It's easy to get seduced by technology, but if real meetings are often not very productive, why should a simulated one be any more so?

- How do you fairly compensate team members who may be making equal contributions to a global project, but are based in very different economies?

So there are potential problems, but also there are opportunities: real meetings and teams are often plagued by boredom, politicking, in-fighting, repetition and more. Rather than just digitising current practice, there are substantial opportunities to invent far better methods. In fact, virtual team processes may actually *improve* on group productivity even if you are all based on the same site. For more on this, see Chapter Thirteen: 'Are Virtual Teams Better Than 'Real' Ones?'

### The nature of the relationship between talent and the business

Peter Drucker once commented that management in the 21st century will be more like marketing: and that's not just at the recruitment stage, but for the duration of the relationship. It's fashionable to talk about a war for talent. Whatever you call it, in any economy, there will always be competition for people who can make valuable contributions. It will pervade the organization and include:

- Your web presence, both formal and informal
- Recruitment and selection
- Assignments
- Consensus-building
- Organizational change
- Parting company
- Alumni networks

The unimaginative response to retaining talent and keeping that talent happy is a salary war. But that's clearly not sustainable, and more creative approaches are going to be required. In short, viable and effective talent retention is going to have to look a lot like building and maintaining brand loyalty among customers.

## Emerging markets reduce potential for competing on costs and features, increasing the importance of design and creating high-value "experiences"

I recently attended a tour of the Birmingham School of Jewellery. It turns out it's the second largest in the world (the biggest is a very different, family run business in Tokyo). The director explained a major difference in the pricing of jewellery East to West. In the East, "bling" jewellery is favoured and the major determinant of price is the breakdown value of the component gems and precious metals. By contrast, the approach he is advocating at conferences is to price items based on the value added by the design – it can be far above the value of the broken-down components.

Standing in the Birmingham Jewellery Quarter in the traditional heart of the British "metal-bashing" industry, this thoughtful, enthusiastic educator was pointing at the need to think in terms of value-pricing, and in particular to the value-creating power of *design* (not a revelation to Apple's Steve Jobs, of course).

**Client satisfaction in services is not about service**

I was talking to a venture capitalist about the lawyers he used. I was interested because I have worked a lot with law firms, and this VC often engaged the services of one of my clients, as well as two of their fiercest competitors. His view of the competition was vastly different to that of the lawyers. His take:

"In the top-tier level, they are all the same in terms of fees, technical know-how, service, even on the quality of our relationship with them. What they don't grasp is that the only real differentiator available to them is their ability to bring me *deals*. I may love my lawyers at XYZ LLP, but if the guy from ABC is bringing me the deals, I'm not going to give XYZ the work out of a sense of loyalty. The firms are really missing a trick. They should be running highly-publicised investment competitions – like (the popular UK TV show) *Dragon's Den* for example – anything to make them a magnet for deals which they can then trade with us."

In fact, some of the most interesting law firms in the UK are following one of two strategies: either they are optimising for very transactional work, or they are carving out high-end niches based on finding out what the client will really respond to – e.g. deal flow for VCs – and then organizing to give it them.

The danger, as in all strategy, lies in falling between two stools: in this case by hoping that the former mystique of their professions and nice tea cups will continue to command a premium, while neither optimising to deliver cheap reliable commodities, nor really understanding their clients' *business* (rather than purely technical) needs.

# What Won't Change

## Execution skills

Charan and Bossidy's book *Execution* was a well-timed return to reality after the dotcom bubble, and also caught the post 9/11 mood. Perhaps it felt safer to focus on internal processes than on grand strategy for a time. And actually, as the name suggests, execution is what executives are supposed to do. Although what it involves isn't sexy, Charan and Bossidy found a sexy word for it.

I think that, like flared jeans (albeit rebranded as bootcut or whatever), execution will always come back in when there's a "correction".

How else are you going to make sure you fulfil your promise to the customer?

## Delegation

So often badly done, and yet with such potential. Imagine if you could measure the outcome of each delegated transaction: did the delegator obtain from the delegatee the result required, at the time required, within the resource constrains required etc.? What if you could improve the average score by 10% throughout your organization? What about 30%? Improving delegation is a high value proposition for a lot of organizations. Let's spell out the benefits.

*The delegator:*

- achieves more, through leverage
- can attend to priorities instead of fire-fighting
- can create better life balance
- develops their executive skills
- creates an excellent context for developing subordinates

## The delegatee:

- learns to take on greater accountability
- acquires the opportunity to learn from more experienced executives
- grows in the confidence required to take on leadership roles

Remember: the key to delegation is to delegate ends, not means. Get people to accept responsibility for producing a result, subject to a satisfactory negotiation for the resources and support they require in order to do so. See Chapter Sixteen for my delegation formula: "REWARDS".

## Collaboration and team-working

While many people can talk a good talk about team-work, collaboration and breaking down silos, there will always be a need for people to understand the potential dysfunctions of groups working together and to have ways to circumvent them so that the benefits can be reached. Issues which remain with us for the long term, include:

- Ways to head off dangerous 'Groupthink'
- Facilitation skills for leaders and internal consultants
- Process improvement through virtual team technology, especially forums
- Team-building on substantive tasks, not on the basis of dubious inventories of personality "types" or abstract "roles"
- Ways to accelerate execution across departmental silos.

## Leadership

Leadership is too often talked about as a mystical quality, and treated as a panacea for all organizational ills. "Leadership problems" can be a lazy diagnosis.

Good leadership behaviours (which can to a large extent be both learned and improved) are a necessary, but not sufficient, component of organizational performance. The most pragmatically useful approaches will emphasise flexibility of behaviour, and an eye to subordinate development.

As important is the cultivation of good "followership": the ability to accept accountability, delegation, and delivery of results.

And the most important leadership principle of all will always be the same: *lead from the front.*

## Your business doesn't have to be original – but pay attention to the customer's experience

Although the terms "customer experience" and "experiential brands" are relatively new, the idea most certainly is not, and I think it has always been at least tacitly understood by successful businesses. In Chapter Six, I talk about the Electric Cinema: it shows the same movies as other places, but the art deco ambiance, homemade cakes, sofas, and staff who are movie buffs create an experience for which customers are willing to pay a premium.

Some key points:

- There's no substitute for the basics – a reliable product trumps a great help desk.

- Outsourcing/offshoring makes customer experience much more difficult to control.

- Starting with the experiences your customers and clients most value, you can "reverse engineer" your operations to fulfil them. It's a neat bridge between strategy and execution.

**Short-termism is the enemy of brand equity**

Seeking quick wins is a good tactic for building momentum and confidence behind a new initiative. But it's not much of a strategy.

How many businesses have carelessly encouraged managers to kill their brands with tricks such as off-shoring customer service to a mediocre call centre to get a "quick win" on the bottom line? Contrary to what most of the customers think, these managers aren't stupid for not knowing what will happen – because they *do* know. They *know* it will harm the brand in the medium term as customers are irritated and turned off. But *they don't care*. Because they will have moved to another job by the time the backlash comes.

Those much-maligned financial traders have a name for this: *IBGYBG* ("I'll be gone; you'll be gone").

## *Final Thoughts*

Clearly human nature doesn't change that much – Greek tragedies, Shakespeare and Machiavelli offer good evidence of that – and so much of what we know about leadership, organization, politics, influence and so on are relatively constant. But technology, economics, politics and demographics do change the reference points and require that organizational know-how be re-jigged and reinterpreted by leaders pretty much continuously (and of course each new generation of managers has to be educated from scratch).

The trick is to know which things to keep doing the same and which changes to respond to.

## OPENNESS TO REALITY

Apparently, a frog thrown into hot water will jump straight out, but the same frog put in cold water that is slowly heated will remain in its nice warm bath until it is boiled alive (who thinks of these things? Worse, who tests them?). The lesson both for frogs and for people is that it can be dangerous to disregard current realities for the sake of short term comfort.

Here are some everyday examples: people procrastinate endlessly about a manager whose behaviour is causing poor morale or high turnover; or they take their own staff's word that the firm's service is considered excellent, rather than asking their clients or customers; or they get defensive when someone points to a potential competitive weakness, rather than reviewing and if necessary adjusting their strategic position.

This kind of evasion may be somewhat effective as a short-term (and short-sighted) anti-stress measure, and I think we all have the tendency from time to time, but in business – as in survival – it can be fatal.

What can be done about it? We can start by offering a model of more effective behaviour ourselves. This might mean:

- Confronting poor performance rather than hoping it will get better on its own (more on an effective way to do that in the essay "The Columbo Technique" on page 194).

- Showing that we are capable of facing uncomfortable facts ourselves, rather than shooting the messenger.

- Calling a client or customer and asking if there is something you should know about your service that you may not know. Doing the same with two to three frontline employees.

- Displaying a willingness to disagree and be disagreed with – to worry less about *who's* right, and more about *what's* right.

- Encouraging ourselves and others to look for evidence that *disconfirms*, rather than supports, bolsters or "sexes up" our current assumptions.

It's almost a truism that these are uncertain and turbulent times. And so it's always a good idea to be open to news of what might be heating up around you.

## IN DEFENCE OF THE "S" WORD

I once gave a talk at a showcase for various regional chairmen of a CEO networking organization. The talk was about the crucial leadership skill of aligning people with strategy. At the end of the talk, one of the leaders said: "I like this, but you'd be better to call this 'culture' rather than 'strategy' – our members don't like strategy".

I can understand the frustration if the term strategy is associated with 'slick' consultants and academics cosseted by tenure (and I'm speaking as a former academic who is now a consultant). But I worry that this attitude simply betrays a reluctance to think before acting – anyone who thinks you can swap the word culture for the word strategy is not thinking much.

I don't think it's such a good idea to pander to the proponents of the "Just do something" approach. After all, they tend to end up like boxers whose defence consists merely of being good at taking punches.

To state a theme which will come up again, you need to be strategic, because:

- There are more things that you *could* do than you *should* do.
- Any effective business project needs to reach a critical mass – you can't spread your resources too thinly.
- You don't know how long current conditions will continue. How long will there even be a market for your current offerings?
- There are loads of risky, hard-to-reverse decisions to be made in any business (which projects? capital investments? hires?) and you need a way to make those commitments that has a good chance of allowing you to survive, let alone thrive.

Maybe these observations point to the real reason why business people often loathe strategy: dealing with these questions means hassle, potential turf wars, and the discomfort of hard thinking.

Willingness to do some hard thinking and debating is vital, however, unless you want to risk:

- Diffusion of effort and resources
- Profitable lines carrying unprofitably ones (possibly without you even realising)
- Tying up unnecessary working capital
- A market which simply fails to appreciate the value you are offering
- Your people making haphazard decisions which inadvertently fight each other
- Getting into a "how low can you go?" limbo competition on prices

Your job as a business leader is surely to create value, for your customers, your investors and your employees. To do that with any predictability requires strategy.

## CHAPTER FOUR

# WHAT'S A STRATEGY FOR?

There seem to be hundreds of definitions of strategy, and as many approaches to strategy formulation. They range from inspiring "How I Did It" accounts by star CEOs, to matrices and charts from the large consultancies, heavily financial models from accountancy firms, weighty books from the business school academics, through to flimsy SWOT analyses in paperbacks available from the "Heathrow Business School" (i.e. World News at Terminal 3).

Actually there are many ways to set a useful strategy. More important than the precise method used is whether or not your strategy is producing the goods. The real question is *how would you know if your strategy was working?* In other words, the thing is to shift the emphasis away from inputs to the process (e.g. complicated methodologies) and towards outputs i.e. valuable results).

Rather than defining strategy, I think it's simpler and much more useful to define the *purpose* of a strategy. At its most basic, it answers the questions:

- What products and/or services will we sell?
  - o  ... and *not* sell?

- Who will we sell them to?
  - o  ... and *not* sell them to?

- Why should they spend their money with *us*,
  - o  ... rather than with someone else?

## Questions to Test for Strategic Understanding

Here's a way of provoking useful discussion on the value of your strategy. A good strategy should enable people to answer the following sorts of questions. (Even if they need to refer to other people for the details, the strategy should be clear enough for them to get broadly the right answer on their own.)

**For the senior team**

Can you answer, or at least have a focused and confident discussion about, the following questions:

- Should we enter this market?
- Stay in this market?
- Go with this product?
- Pursue innovation in this area?

And can you do so without descending into an overly-detailed discussion of current operating constraints?

A lack of strategic focus often shows up as a proliferation of products, services, customer types or brands. Over the last few years, companies as varied as Sony, Unilever and GM have had to deal with the consequences of such proliferation. They've experienced stretched development and marketing resources, and difficulty putting enough money behind those products in which they should be investing. I've seen the proliferation problem in all kinds of organizations (and in individual careers). It causes huge waste and demoralisation, and it can only be sorted out by knowing what business you are in, and what business you are not.

A good strategy also needs to be capable of actually being executed. It should provide the confident starting point for knowing:

- What needs to happen in order for us to meet our vision of the future? What do we need to plan for?

- How are people, operations, finance and markets linked so as to produce sustained increases in value?

*Benefits of clear strategy for the senior team include:* Clarity, leading to better resource allocation, profitability and return to shareholders (for those wanting guidance on methods, we'll look in more depth at questions of product and market mix Chapter Eight *Driving Strategic Priorities*).

## For customer-facing staff

A key component of a clear strategy is a well-understood value proposition. This is one of the best ways to enhance customer service and employee empowerment. Do your staff have a way to answer questions of the following sort with confidence?

- How do I handle this particular *non-standard* customer issue?

For example, I know a client of FedEx whose package had missed its (FedEx-operated) flight. The person at the call centre asked him "What do you want to do?" He said, "Well I thought your promise was something like *'when it absolutely, positively has to be there overnight'*." She said, "Oh, I see what you mean. I'm sorry to trouble you, sir. We'll pay for it to go on a United flight." Clearly she did the right thing because she and her customer shared an understanding of the FedEx customer story – a key part of their strategy.

*Benefits of clear strategy for customers and service staff:* Provides conditions in which staff can be safely empowered and given autonomy. Improves customer experience. Improves employee satisfaction.

## For decision makers at all levels

Strategy is not just a once-a-year issue for senior team retreats. People throughout the organization – in sales, in R&D, in customer service to mention three – are constantly faced with questions which can take the business towards or away from your intended strategy (for example, by continuing to pursue easy sales opportunities in markets you have decided to abandon, by developing pet technologies you can't commercialise, or by undermining your brand by over- or under-serving the customer).

So, do your people have a way to know, on a day-to-day basis:

- What of the many things I could do, should I do?

- What historical activities do I need to stop doing?

- How can I demonstrate that I and my people are making a valuable contribution to the organization?

*Benefits of clear strategy for organization-wide decision-makers:* Increased coordination, better "time management", reduced cul-de-sacs and non-aligned work.

## For shareholders (of a profit-making enterprise)

Investors need to be confident that they are likely to see a return, and your strategy is the key to the story that will give them that confidence. If the story doesn't hang together, they will be very unhappy. Interestingly, not only must you know what you are doing, but you need to be seen to know. One new chief executive of a manufacturing company decided the business needed a comprehensive review before any big decisions were made, and told his private equity investors that it was "too soon" for him to have a strategy. They wrongly concluded that he was letting things drift, and gave him a hard time in the meeting. On reflection, he realised that although he knew what he was doing, they needed to hear a more compelling story before they could accept it. When he came back to them outlining a series of "strategic experiments" they were delighted. The questions they, and all rational investors, need a good answer to from you strategy is quite simply:

- Does this company seem likely to offer a good return in the future?

Of course, to answer that question they may need all kinds of supplementary information about things such as likely revenues, margins, cashflows and so on. And by the way, don't get too hung up on the minutiae of projecting figures – always an exercise in fantasy – think first about the customer story: is it sufficiently compelling to get you those revenues and margins?

*Benefits of clear strategy for attracting investors:* Ongoing, perhaps increased, investment, support for enhanced share price.

### For trustees and funders (of a non-profit)

The forgoing considerations are similar when it comes to non-profits, especially as governments look to these organizations to be increasingly sustainable without so much public money:

- Does the organization seem likely to maintain its viability while delivering increasing value to its beneficiaries?

*Benefits:* Helps meet governance responsibilities and encourages funding.

## For supply chain partners

A look at the strategies of some automotive manufacturers in the UK caused a number of their suppliers to branch out into aerospace and medical equipment – many that didn't or couldn't diversify are now out of business. Supply chain partners are interested in your strategy because they need to know:

- Is this business going to be able to continue to buy (or deliver) what I need?

- Will they be able to pay me?

- What should I be offering them in order to help them meet *their* future customers' needs?

- Can I depend on them as a part of my own planning?

- Will our relationship be cooperative or adversarial?

- How will they work with my people, and (if a supplier) especially my customers?

*Benefits:* Builds trust and credibility, helps protect valuable capabilities and work streams, and informs prudent risk management.

## For providers of internal services

It is easy for providers of internal services to lose sight of the outside world and the interaction with the environment that gives the organization its purpose. I meet far too many disengaged people within organizations who have never met a customer and don't understand or appreciate the fundamental source of the organization's revenue. Whose fault is this? I believe the responsibility is with senior management who fail to articulate an engaging employee story.

Clear strategy should make the link between internal processes and external results by providing answers to the following types of questions:

- What do my internal customers need in order to deliver to our external ones?

- What will they need in the future?

- How do I prioritise provision of internal services?

*Benefits:* Breaks down silos and improves collaboration, encourages engagement and a feeling of being relevant, of participating in value creation and not just "putting in time".

## For IT and infrastructure

To use the terminology of Chapter Eight, most IT people have a "technology" driving force, when what they really need is a "market need" driving force. Therefore they tend to implement systems that do things "because they can" rather than because it meets a specific user requirement. Just look at the various increasingly bloated versions of Microsoft Word for a rich example.

The other thing about IT projects is that they tend to be late. All the more reason to help your IT people anticipate your needs so that they can get started early. The overall question your strategy should be helping them with is:

- Are we going to have the right systems and information in the right places at the right times to continue to deliver increasing value on a sustained basis?

*Benefits:* Viability, control of project costs, increased accountability of system development activities.

**For HR, succession planning, talent management**

If there was a hit parade for corporate B.S. (i.e. statements made with apparent sincerity, then contradicted by evidence observable to everyone), the chart-topper would surely be: "People are our greatest resource." It's one of those statements you are supposed to agree with, but I suspect that many harbour the guilty secret that they don't buy it. What we end up with then is an almost ideological split between "people" people, and "numbers" people. I suggest you reject this either/or debate, and simply ask and carefully answer the following question in the context of your specific business:

- Are we going to have the right people in the right places at the right times to continue to deliver increasing value on a sustained basis?

*Benefits:* Viability, control of salary costs, increased accountability of learning and development activities

## Application To Your Business

Test yourselves: can the relevant people answer the relevant questions correctly *without having to ask anyone else?*

The potential dangers of having an unclear strategy are found in reversing the benefits above, for example:

- Confusion about objectives
- Inefficient resource allocation
- Disappointing profitability and return to shareholders
- Increased vulnerability to competitors, economic changes
- People wasting resources on non-aligned work.
- Proliferation of unprofitable products and services
- Staff who lack initiative on behalf of customers

- Dissatisfied employees
- Silos and turf wars
- Inadequate succession planning
- Lack of accountability of learning and system development activities

## *Final Thoughts*

It can take some courage to test people with the questions in this chapter. If they can't answer at least broadly correctly off the top of their heads, some form of strategy work could be in order – start by revisiting your three stories!

Even successful, growing organizations have to keep on top of this – the environment changes constantly and strategy has to evolve to keep pace. The answers to the questions need to change over time. Will your people continue to answer correctly?

*What's a Strategy for?*

# CHAPTER FIVE

# ORGANIC GROWTH
# STEP BY STEP

*(Based on an article co-written with Alastair Dryburgh)*

Let's suppose you have identified the products, services and markets with the greatest potential, you have a plan showing the costs and revenues involved, you know what everyone needs to be doing, and everyone is committed and raring to go... You are now at the point where most growth initiatives start to fail.

In the military they say: "no plan survives contact with the enemy". This chapter looks at how to ensure that your plan for growth survives contact with reality.

Let's assume that you have the prerequisites – you have a product or service that the market wants, and the capabilities to produce it economically and sell it effectively. Even once you have those, there are financial and people pitfalls on the way to profitable growth.

Here are the top six suggested by experience:

## 1. When the going gets tough, the tough get distracted

When unforeseen events arise, *as they inevitably will from time to time,* proactive initiatives get put on hold while people fight the fires. Once the blaze is out, people have been distracted and the growth plan never recovers momentum. How many strategy documents sit gathering dust, never to see full implementation, because of this phenomenon?

## 2. Buying-in to the plan leads to getting 'whacked'

People find that they are inadvertently *punished* for attempting to implement the new plans. For example, a group of associates in a property consultancy were participating in a project to boost business development. Those who enthusiastically embraced it and began actively marketing and networking soon realised that they were doing so for no extra reward (actually to their loss of time) relative to their colleagues who stayed in the office clocking up billable hours.

## 3. Growth inadvertently feeds unprofitable (loss-making?) activities

Most businesses have unprofitable bits to them: you need to be sure that you aren't energetically growing those! Before you go for growth, get accurate data to ensure you identify any loss-making customers, products, services, types of project etc. Be prepared for surprise and disbelief. You can sometimes get profit growth just by dropping activities.

## 4. Vested interests protect themselves with lip-service commitments

People have agreed to the growth plan – you think they are on board so you commit to your plan – but they have no intention of following through because their current safety is threatened. Example: sales managers who really need to delegate to their sales force may be reluctant to give up key customer relationships that they see as a hedge against future employment uncertainty. They can't really admit this and appear super-agreeable to new proposals in your planning and strategy meetings. This kind of stalling can go on quite happily for quarter after quarter.

## 5. There are a lot of financial plates to keep spinning – it's easy to drop one

Most growth has to be financed out of operations – it's likely to be very difficult to raise more money to do it. This means looking hard at the profitability of the existing business. As you achieve growth, you may find it has unfavourable cashflow implications which you need to anticipate and deal with. Therefore, you need a cushion to protect your growth plans when things get tight – if you are doing "just well enough" now, that won't be enough when you start to grow.

## 6. There's a disconnect between the financial and the behavioural

Unless they are very disciplined, each member of a management team will tend to look at the growth challenge through their own lens, according to their background. This then drives the positions they take in discussions. For example, financial types will, hopefully, caution against overtrading, sales and marketing folk will emphasise top-line growth, organization development types will promote the importance of empowerment and delegation. In far too many cases, each type fails to heed the wisdom being offered by their "team-mates", sometimes to the point of being dismissive and rude. It's amazing how easily people take an argument *for* the importance of another aspect of the business as a criticism *against* their own area. In fact, each of these areas, and some others, must be balanced if growth is to result.

## *Growth Step by Step*

So how do you use these insights to grow your business step by step?

### Decide what's worth growing

If you are looking to grow profits (as opposed to revenue or staff numbers), recognise that some parts of the business shouldn't grow, and in fact they should probably shrink. Avoid emulating the major telecoms company who grew rapidly but then turned suddenly through 180 degrees when they realised that 80% of their customers were losing them money. They had been chasing growth in revenues or market share, without sufficient attention to profitability. They ended up with 89% of their customers generating just 4% of their revenues and 2% of their gross margins. Allowing for the operating costs involved in supporting those customers, they were clearly losing money.

It can be hard work – and you may need to bring in external help – but you must understand which of your products, market channels and customers make you good profits, which barely pay their way and which lose money. Without this knowledge, any general exhortations to "Go for Growth" could lead you off in exactly the wrong direction.

And look at cashflow as well as profit. Growth tends to suck in a lot of working capital, and positive cashflow may not show up for an appreciable time after you reach profitability. Carelessly managed growth can easily create survival issues.

### Create some surplus profitability

Substantial growth takes time and money. Most businesses are pretty lean these days (maybe too lean, but that's another story). You are unlikely to have people and resources standing around doing nothing, so unless you want to take big risks with your existing business (the last thing to do when you are trying to grow), growth will need extra people and extra costs. Most of the time, you will need to find these inside the existing business.

How are you going to reshape the existing business to fund growth? If you have done the work required from step one, there are three main ways to do it:

- **Eliminate activities which are losing money.** There are probably some of those, and if they can't be fixed, you can boost profits simply by stopping them.

- **Identify the customers who are losing you money and fix them.** If you know that a customer, or type of customer, is losing you money, it is not hard to renegotiate. Simply being happy to walk away if you can't get a better deal means you probably won't have to – they will sense your confidence and fall into line.

- **Reallocate resources towards more profitable activities.** Once you know how your total profit breaks down by product, channel or customer, look at whether your sales, marketing and service budgets break down in the same proportion. They may well not – more likely the best resources are allocated to the biggest problems, not the biggest opportunities. Putting this right will boost profitability.

Be sure to create not just the profitability you need to fund the plan, but also a cushion to protect it in the event that other things go wrong, as they inevitably will.

## Create a transition plan

The best way to plan a transition is to start with a picture of *what things will look like when they are finished*. Imagine you are the subject of a documentary about the successful changes you have wrought. What would you be showing the interviewer and crew to illustrate the results? Answering this question will make the aim tangible, and will tell you a lot about the activities required to achieve it.

Then answer the supplementary question: what is the organization going to be like *while it is going through* the transition? This question, rarely considered, is important because much so-called resistance to change is actually fear of uncertainty. If people have a sense of the ultimate destination (for buy-in) and some idea of what it will be like on the way, things will go more smoothly.

To flesh the plan out, make sure that you:

- Create appropriate KPIs for new activities: what will be the observable evidence that things are going in the right direction?
- Decide who does what, and get their commitment.
- Ensure that they have the resources necessary in order to deliver.

### Build in plan protection

Growth efforts are sometimes built merely on wishful thinking, bullying and finger-crossing. Chest-beaters often rise in organizations, but that sometimes means that they have a bigger ship to crash into the rocks.

The most important part of a plan (the part that often isn't there) is the risk analysis. You can keep the format very simple:

- What could go wrong?
- How likely is it?
- How serious would it be if it happened?
- What do we do to prevent it?
- How do we prepare to deal with it if it happens?

As simple as this analysis is, the point is to do it.

## Create leverage of your management time

You are going to need more people, and you are going to need to be able to delegate more to them (there's a format for the mechanics of delegation on page 173).

Additional bodies can be paid for using the surplus profitability you created earlier. But more people don't automatically lead to increased productivity. Indeed, the pioneering software engineer Fred Brooks formulated Brook's Law ("Adding manpower to a late software project makes it later") in the mid-1970s, but I find contemporary implementation teams who have never heard of it. It's not just true in systems implementation: more people means greater communication overhead, more confusion potential, and a greater decision-making bottleneck in the shape of the leader. Creating a culture of effective delegation is vital if your additional expenditure is to be worthwhile.

Without delegation, growth is impossible, as millions of exhausted would-be entrepreneurs demonstrate. And, in addition to the personal barriers about losing control that leaders often need to overcome, there are two others. Firstly, what about the willingness of their reports to accept delegated accountability? And then, *they* must also be able to delegate to the next level – or else you've just swapped one limit (the capacity of the leader) for another (the capacity of the leader plus that of their direct reports – more, for sure, but still a restrictive limit).

Good delegation is a coaching process, not the one-off assignment, or worse, abdication, of responsibility. Ultimately the aim should be to educate people about the links between their behaviours, drivers of business results, and overall business ROI. i.e. to share your overall strategy and the KPIs, and to make sure everyone has an indicator which tells them how well they are contributing.

## Get the indicators right

Developing suitable key performance indicators for growing businesses (or new lines of business in a larger organization) can be problematic. Many established businesses are run with few indicators beyond the profit and loss account, but this won't help you in the early stages. You can't hold people to normal standards of profitability in the early days, but releasing them from that discipline can result in disappointing results. All this means you are going to need a range of measures to make sure you are staying on track.

Two very good indicators are cost of customer acquisition and lifetime customer value. You may be losing money in the new business because you don't have enough sales to cover fixed costs, but if you see that you can acquire customers at an average cost of £10,000 and they make you £50,000 over a likely three year lifetime, you have a good basis for continuing to invest. If on the other hand the cost of acquisition is £30,000 and the value is £25,000, no amount of growth will bring you to profitability.

Other KPIs to consider include:

- Whether project milestones are being hit
- The percentage of prospects who convert into customers
- The percentage of first time customers who buy again
- The proportion of customers who fit the "ideal customer" profile you identified when you started

## Make sure you really are incentivizing the right things

This may seem obvious, but if there is a formal incentive system, make sure that it promotes the efforts needed for growth. The incentives need to be based on the indicators you are using for the new business.

In Chapter Five, I talk about the property consultancy associates who threw themselves enthusiastically into networking activities but then equally quickly lost their enthusiasm. Building business relationships one person at a time is crucial for many professional advisors, but it takes a while to yield results. Those who bought into the initiative were sincere in their efforts. Meanwhile, however, their less energetic colleagues were achieving much more flattering utilisation rates (on which they were rewarded) by eschewing business development and staying in the office to work on existing, but finite, projects. If business development one-to-one is important, people have to benefit by attempting it.

Once the formal incentives are properly aligned, you need to see if there are any less tangible factors pulling people in the wrong direction. For example:

- People who don't feel competent to take on new roles

- Salespeople who don't want to relinquish day to day contact with accounts (these relationships are their long term job security)

Finally, realise that most people, when under stress, tend to revert to old patterns of behaviour. You need a way to spot when this starts to happen and correct it.

## Don't abdicate behaviour change to trainers

As a business grows, people will naturally be required to do new things. When behaviour change is required, the solutions often attempted are to either issue edicts or provide training. The first of these is extremely hit-and-miss: I remember a senior civil servant bemoaning his own boss's naiveté about management with the memorable phrase: "He seems to regard a memo as a proxy for action."

The second response, training, is widely misapplied, with disappointing results. Training is a limited intervention because it only addresses abstract skills (which are *potential* behaviours and no more). Let's consider the case of delegation as an example. People can easily learn the required skills in a workshop or coaching session and demonstrate in a case study that they have enough understanding to apply it.

Nonetheless, delegation training seminars may have little or no effect in creating the desired leverage. If a reluctant delegator has the attitude that they will only be credible to their bosses if they know every tiny implementation detail within their purview, then their delegating skills are effectively disabled. No amount of skill building will help such a person unless it also addresses their attitude. And to do this it will almost certainly have to address the attitude-shaping power of culture.

*The key is that there is a cultural override* which is more powerful than requests, instructions or indeed training. When a training course is effective, for example, you can be sure that the culture already supports the desired behaviours, or that someone (managers, trainers, consultants) made adjustments to the culture in sync with the training.

The most elegant leverage point for changing organization-wide behaviour is to change the behaviour of those from whom everyone else takes their cues: it can be a formal boss, but it may equally be an informal leader, top performer or charismatic individual contributor. Identify these people and get them on board first, and behaviour change initiatives, including training, will have a much greater impact.

## *Final Thoughts*

An awful lot of businesses proceed in fits and starts, enjoying one or more periods of growth, then getting comfortable and ending up on a plateau. Having lost momentum, the next spurt only comes after a shock or injection of energy from the outside.

Here's a leadership challenge: What if, in contrast, you build an organization where a continuing process of growth and innovation is standard operating procedure – an organization where the disciplines of growth are part of your day to day business, not something that gets turned on and off when external events leave no choice?

Later in the book, we will look at ways to address the internal challenges of building a high-performance culture, but let's not get ahead of ourselves. Growth can ultimately come from only one source: providing more value to customers.

# CHAPTER SIX

# THE IMPORTANCE OF
# CUSTOMER EXPERIENCE IS
# NOTHING NEW...
# BUT IT IS IMPORTANT

There's a great cinema in Birmingham called the
Electric. It's been a favourite of mine for years and,
although it's changed a lot (including in ownership),
it's kept, and continued to develop, a certain sense of
the Electric Cinema experience. There was always a
home-made cake and coffee shop (rather that hotdogs
and popcorn), and the people who served you were
movie buffs – one was actually the projectionist. Now
it's had a refurbishment there are sofas in the cinema
and you can text your cake order to the shop during
the movie. You can go and see the same film there or
at the Odeon, but it's a very different experience.

I read recently that "customer experience" is the
new battleground. Hmm, well maybe. A lot of what
I'm seeing said by people on customer *experience* is
what they were saying last year about customer
*service*. They've just done a global "search and
replace" on all their copy.

So, is this is a notion that's going to be practically
useful, or just a way of sexing up an old area? I think
for most it'll be the latter. But I also think that a key
factor in great businesses is that they, like the Electric
Cinema, have always created great experiences (both
in your interaction with them, and in your use of their
product or service).

And as competition from emerging markets hots
up and western businesses look for ways to stay

viable (and ideally create new ways to deserve a premium), it's an extremely useful way of thinking about your value proposition, about how design enhances that value and what it takes to deliver it on a consistent basis.

Below I'll provide a six step plan for using the idea of the customer's experience as a bridge between strategy and its successful execution. But first, let's repel those boarders looking to jump on another buzzword bandwagon.

## *No Silver Bullet*

Before we get carried away, a few observations:

- **Attention to the "experience" is no substitute for good basics.** I recently saw a video lecture on "experiential brands" which held up the Apple stores as a leading example. I browsed a bit for more info and found a really insightful comment to the effect that "Sure the Apple store help-desk staff are really cool, but I'd just prefer it if my iPod didn't break down in the first place..."

- **Experience is just another name for service.** Here we find a slew of cut-and-paste artists who are swapping the word "service" for the word "experience", in much the same way as they renamed the steward running the train's buffet as the "retail services manager". Many of the customer service practices we are subjected to by call centres actually worsen our experience – a lot of older people hate being called by their first names by kids of their grandchildren's age, for example. Listen to people complain about call-centre service: what they often want is experiential: a feeling of being given some time, some respect, and – a crucial issue for financial service institutions – advice from someone who inspires confidence that they actually know what they are talking about and are not just reading a script. How do you create the essential elements of that experience for your customers?

- **You can't just bolt it on.** If you put the average nightclub doorman in a dinner suit (tuxedo) and get him to call guests "Sir", it still sounds menacing – sometimes more so because of the incongruity (of course, this is where the customer experience game gets subtle: that sense of menace might actually provide a frisson that customers value). This sense of the deeper experience is where truly thoughtful design makes the difference. Bolt-on wings and go-faster stripes don't even get you close to the elegance of a car styled by Pininfarina.

- **Many businesses have part of it, but are not consistent**. I booked a ticket for Amtrak from Manhattan to Rhode Island. I did it three weeks in advance from a computer in a suburb of Birmingham, UK at 11.30 pm on a Friday night – it took eight or nine minutes. When I arrived at Penn Station and inserted my credit card into the machine it said (without any further action on my part) "Welcome, Dr Bass" and printed my tickets. It was worthy of the 1970s sci-fi films I was brought up on, and I experienced quite a kick from it. Then I tried to understand from the attendant how to check in my luggage… A Wookie from *Star Wars* would have been more helpful.

## *Six Steps to Innovative Customer Experience*

Here's a six step process for using the customer experience idea to increase differentiation, attract a premium, and align strategy with implementation.

1. **Start by setting aside what you think you know about your products, services and existing processes for the moment**

Too many technical experts expect customers and clients to become sophisticated in their expertise. Over twenty years since he did it with the Apple Mac, Steve Jobs again demonstrated with the iPod and iPhone that people like computing devices that don't act like computing devices. A services example: I hear clients of big-name law firms complaining that their lawyers expect them to pay essentially for essays or lectures on the law, followed by the opportunity to make their own mind up.

If you start with your technology as you see it, you will put constraints on the resulting customer experience. These constraints are at a minimum unnecessary, and are usually dysfunctional, causing lower satisfaction, irritation and choices in favour of the competition if the competition creates better experiences (people pay a premium for iPod often because its user-interface is much easier to use than many other MP3 players – even a 2010 Sony is no match for a mid 2000's iPod).

## 2. What kinds of experiences do your customers value?

Think from the standpoint of your customer or client. Ask fundamental questions. What kind of experiences do they value? This has to be done in a deep way – it's not just a matter of banal customer service phrases such as, "Is there anything else I can help you with today?" What do people need to see, hear, feel, smell and taste in order to have the kind of experience you wish to create for them?

Look for quirky or cult small businesses for examples. I've already mentioned the Electric Cinema: people like the opportunity to watch a film on the big screen, sitting on a comfortable sofa, with the ability to call up coffee and homemade cake at their fingertips.

Another example is Hudson's Restaurant and Gourmet Food Shop, again in Birmingham, a wonderful coffee house inspired by the eccentric sense of style of its founder, a former undertaker (!) looking for a decent cup of coffee. The basic blueprint is that Hudson is a butler a bit like P.G. Wodehouse's Jeeves. The business has lost something as it has expanded: part of its charm used to be tongue-in-cheek (but extremely polite and attentive) service and a mock faded elegance. It's tidier and "straighter" now, although the best of the staff still play up to the role, and it sets the tone. And I'll bet that their gross margin on coffee is higher even than that of the Starbucks across the street.

## 3. Identify the qualities that act as "markers" for the experience

What are the sequences, qualities, tones, colours and interaction patterns that add up to the experience? For example, Hudson's and the Electric Cinema, although providing different services, share some structural elements:

- They have a home-made feel

- They have an eccentric ambiance carrying the stamp of their founder's/owner's personality

- They are very "English" in an old fashioned way: the Electric has a 1920s style art deco façade; Hudson's staff are dressed like waiters and waitresses from an Edwardian tea room

These factors are additional to the fact that Hudson's serves good sandwiches and the Electric has a varied programme of commercial and art house films. Providing them doesn't add noticeable costs vis-à-vis competitors. And while I can see the same film or get as good a sandwich elsewhere, their customers are prepared to pay more, and are happy doing so, at these two places.

## 4. What other experiences and values would be compelling to those people?

If you followed my description of Hudsons and the Electric Cinema, it shouldn't come as a surprise that I and my friends enjoy the Goodwood Revival motor racing event. Although they are very different in content (tea and sandwiches, movies, historic motor racing) they share many of the same structural features which create experiences I find worth paying for. If someone produced a bookshop, or a gym, or a train, with the same elements, I'm pretty sure I'd favour them over all competitors, and pay a premium for it.

That's how you market to me, of course, not to your own customers. But I've found in my own informal research that people generally have this sort of structural template. And further, if you follow the template in packaging a new offering, they'll highly value it.

## 5. What would have to be there, behind the scenes, in order to produce that?

First ask what experience will your customer most value, and then figure out how to deliver it at a profit. "The Turk" was a hoax, the work of Wolfgang von Kempelen in the 18th century, which purported to be a chess-playing automaton. It consisted of a wooden cabinet behind which was seated a mannequin dressed in a cloak and turban. Opening the cabinet doors revealed internal clockwork mechanisms and, when activated, the mechanism appeared to be able to play a strong game of chess against a human opponent. In reality, the cabinet was cleverly constructed to allowed a (small) chess master to hide inside and operate the mannequin.

Von Kempelen, like the Wizard of Oz, and stage magicians through the ages, understood all about customer experience! He started by figuring out the interaction that would impress the client, then worked out a mechanism to deliver it.

Not quite as exciting, but when I started my career in software engineering we took much the same approach to developing user interfaces. We would develop the user interaction (customer experience) first, animating it using a "fake" mechanism, until people were happy with the interaction style. Only then would we figure out the programming needed to deliver the full functionality of the system on a consistent basis.

Once you understand the experience your customer will value, you then reverse engineer the processes to produce it. In this way, you link strategy to execution. Before Disney introduced their retail stores, they build a prototype on an empty studio lot on the advice of Steve Jobs. They tinkered with it until the experience was just right. Only then did they roll the design out.

## 6. Monitor it, and treat it as a work-in-progress

Once you have a mechanism that generates the intended experience on a consistent basis, establish a feedback loop with customers. Use their responses to improve and evolve the quality of the experience. Surveys and focus groups are useful, but they can introduce noise, as well. Like Lord Seiff, mystery shop your operation yourself. Follow customers around and observe them. That will give you a much better sense of the experience, as well as helping you assess the results of more formal research.

At the same time, you can use process improvement methods to look for increasingly efficient, reliable and/or robust ways to organize the back-end processes.

In this way, the experience your customer has provides a link between your strategy and your execution that drives innovation and simultaneously allows people to understand clearly how their personal contributions add to the whole enterprise.

## *Final Thoughts*

Ultimately, all value has to be experienced directly by someone through their senses. If you are to deliver value, you have to deliver experiences. As mind-bending as it can be, it is therefore highly rewarding to think about your business *from the outside*; as if the business was a theatre and you were living through the experience it creates. Then ask yourself – would my target customer pay for this?

---

### HOW MOMENTS OF TRUTH SHAPE YOUR BUSINESS

Recently, while paying for shopping in Waitrose, I asked the checkout assistant for change for a tenner "while she had the till open". She said it was no problem, but could I please do it at Customer Service on my way out, who would be happy to help me. Customer Service was being staffed by a supervisor, who cheerfully informed me that the check-out assistant had said something that was against their policy, *but that she would give me change anyway because that was what I had been promised.*

I was impressed by a supervisor making good on the promise of an entry-level, part-time employee. Even though that promise was against firm policy, it was in line with their strategy, as it was to the benefit of the customer. It seems clear to me that Waitrose has successfully communicated its strategy and empowered people to act in order to implement it. I have subsequently told a lot of people – individually and in audiences – about my experience, as well as committing it to writing.

#### Strategy succeeds or fails in IMPLEMENTATION

As we have said, setting strategy is generally a tough process, involving much debate and hard choices. After all that effort, it is frustrating if your people then act in a way which undermines your hard-made decisions.

---

Examples:

- A sales director opens up new markets which it would be costly to learn to service. At the same time, they neglect to increase business in existing markets where you can profitably cash in your experience and reputation.

- Overly helpful staff undermine a "no-frills" service strategy by going the extra mile and wiping out margins (going the extra mile makes sense at Waitrose or Fedex, but not at Ryanair).

- Managers promote people who take undue risks with client assets because they earn good returns in the short term (we have seen the results of this in the banking sector, but it goes on all over the place).

**Moments of truth – where strategy becomes action**

The actions of the check-out girl, and particularly the supervisor, were *moments of truth* for Waitrose: times when someone had a decision to make that would lead the business to act in a way that was either aligned or non-aligned with Waitrose's strategy.

Similarly, everyday decisions by staff about which accounts to pursue, who to promote, who to hire, whether to give a refund, all dictate whether or not your business is going to end up moving in the direction you want it to.

**Some questions to consider:**

- What are *your* business's moments of truth?
- What proportion of the time are your people resolving them the way your strategy needs them to?
- How can you tilt the proportion further in your favour?

# CHAPTER SEVEN

# EVERYONE AN INNOVATOR

Talk about innovation, and technological innovation is the one that leaps to most people's minds. And many people incorrectly decide that as they are not in a technology business, innovation isn't really a key issue for them.

| INNOVATION TYPE | WHAT IT IS | ISSUES INCLUDE |
|---|---|---|
| Technology | **Some novel *technology* which enables you to offer a completely new product, service or feature to a customer or client** e.g. new digital storage media, blockbuster drug development. | Large investment required, is risk and return acceptable? Commercialisation challenges: a product is not a business! |
| Process | **Some new or improved *process* within your operation which allows you to offer the current or evolving products or services in a more efficient /effective manner.** e.g. Lean approaches simultaneously improve customer choice/ responsiveness and reduce inventory. | Process improvements are needed to avoid backsliding but are not sufficient for enduring competitive advantage. Does culture support or hinder required behaviour? Relationships with suppliers and customers require care (As my friend Phil Stunell says: "Lean, not mean".) |
| Customer- value/experience | **Some new arrangement of product and service features that enable you to offer much more (ideally "game changing") *value* to the customer even though it uses existing technology** e.g. the recent classic is Apple's iPhone/iTunes – there were MP3 players already, but not an easy way to get access to lots of songs. | Seeing the world and perceiving value the way the customer does. Not being limited by apparently unchangeable bureaucracy and silos. |

Table 7.1: Three types of innovation

Actually, the most valuable innovation opportunities are often *not* technological, even in high tech companies. To show you what I mean, let's identify three types of innovation: technology, process and customer-value (see Table 7.1).

Clearly there is a danger of missing substantial opportunities by interpreting innovation too narrowly. Here are eleven ideas for value-creating innovation in all kinds of businesses.

### 1. Don't think that innovation is just for tech companies

One of my favourite thinkers on the subject of innovation is Peter Selkirk, Chief Executive of Taylor. Why? Well Taylor make bins, and I can't imagine a lower technology than a bin. It's just a container. But Taylor have innovated the ways their bins appear, the way they lock, how easy and safe they are to handle, how they fit into the built environment, and they have even provided consultancy to cities on waste management. Peter dramatically makes the point to our budding entrepreneurs that there are many aspects of a business that contribute value to the customer, not just the latest technology. Other examples: Wetherspoons Pubs, Starbucks Coffee (customer experience) and Coca-Cola (branding).

### 2. If you are a tech company, don't think that innovation is just the tech bit

An invention is not a business. Mouse and windows type computer interfaces were invented at Xerox – but they aren't even in the computer industry now. It took Steve Jobs of Apple to commercialise the idea. Rolls-Royce have phenomenal innovation in turbines, but a key *commercial* innovation has been long-term "power by the hour" contracts (in essence you pay for the thrust your aircraft use, rather than for the jet engines, and RR takes the responsibility for maintaining service). This key insight has helped them weather the current economic downturn so much better than other manufacturers who need to keep selling new engines and parts.

### 3. Value innovation is where the action is in almost all businesses

You cannot take an averagely performing business and create a sustained competitive advantage by cost cutting. You have got to find ways to provide a better ROI to the customer. If you are going to do that by being low cost, then you have to innovate your systems so that nobody can undercut you, like Ryanair do. If that isn't viable, then forget competing purely on cost – look what happened to BA Connect. Instead, focus everyone on how to make sure that the premium that your customers pay (compared to the low-cost leader's price) is *worth it*. This doesn't necessarily mean making big capital expenditures, but it may mean a lot of hard thinking.

### 4. Think about your business from the outside in

Recall from Chapter Six how Disney, on the advice of Board member Steve Jobs, built a mock-up of the Disney Store on an old movie lot and tinkered with it until it felt right. Surveys and interviews with customers can only get you so far – you need to create concrete experiences in order to be sure how people will respond. (There is probably a limit to how far a simulation can do this though. When Tesco started Fresh 'n' Easy in the US, their executives spend months living with typical consumers, and they too built a movie set mock-up. Fresh 'n' Easy has yet to prove itself and while there are a number of possible explanations, including the general economy, one former Tesco executive was quoted in the *Financial Times* as saying, "you only really understand what you

are doing once you open the doors to the store."[2]
Surely a case for an iterative approach to roll-outs.)

## 5. Don't waste time with unstructured brainstorming

Research supports what many of us have learned from experience. Brainstorming in a group usually produces unimpressive ideas. The group has a dampening effect on the creativity of all but the most confident, and nay-sayers jump in prematurely with reasons why something won't work (breaking the rules of brainstorming, but that's what happens). Much better to give people time to come up with ideas individually so they can think them through before presenting them.

## 6. Use deliberate techniques

There are many deliberate techniques for fostering ideas, and we look at a range on the Aston Entrepreneurship Programme. They almost all work better than pure brainstorming because a blank sheet of paper often just triggers a blank state of mind. Innovation requires structure.

## 7. Have systematic ways of turning ideas into reality

The astronomers have a saying: "If it's not written down, it wasn't seen." The business equivalent: "If you can't commercialise an idea, it ain't an innovation." Ideas, good ones, are two a penny. I am sure loads of people independently thought of phones that can surf the internet. But BlackBerry and iPhone led because RIM and Apple commercialised best. If you don't have standard ways to assess ideas against factors such as strategic fit, value to the customer, your ability to implement them, risk-reward and so on, then you

[2] *Tough Times for Tesco's American Dream,* Elizabeth Rigby, FT.com, September 20 2010

need to establish them in order to have any chance of making progress.

## 8. Create a culture where people can take acceptable risks

I hear loads of people bemoaning the lack of entrepreneurialism among their people. But they fail to acknowledge that getting on in an organization is often more a matter of not making mistakes, and not showing their boss up, than it is a matter of creating new value.

## 9. Create a way to run experiments

Sometimes there is just no way to know for sure if an idea is a good one. Rather than having what sounds like a logical argument about the merits without actually having any facts, or searching for more and more data which does nothing to resolve the ambiguity, run some experiments. Strictly define the parameters, decide on kill points, but remember too that you have to spend some money to make money. And remember to reward people who run a competent experiment that doesn't work out – they just saved you a load of money!

## 10. Figure out how to jump on opportunities

Apple's Steve Jobs claims that his strategy is to see what's going on, and then jump on it. That is how he accounts for the iPhone/iTunes phenomenon. But to be able to do this, you have to be ready. When presented with a square centimetre of opportunity, can you seize it? Is your decision process fast enough? Can strategic fit be assessed quickly enough? Can resources be redeployed?

## 11. Instead of emphasising problem-solving in operational areas, emphasise improvement

A problem should not be seen as a cue merely to restore previous performance, yet many people think they are doing a good job as long as they maintain 'business as usual'. The trouble is that the best competitors are working to make business as usual into 'business as it used to be'.

## *All Parts of the Business Can Innovate*

Innovation ought to be of crucial concern to *all* businesses, yet many people think it's just for high-tech firms. Actually high-tech innovation is generally the costliest and highest risk sort of innovation, and many high-tech (and top-notch professional service) businesses have superb products and services which they fail to exploit to their potential, precisely because they don't innovate in processes and especially in value as perceived by the customer or client.

Contrast that with Coca-Cola. It's sugary water. It's not even the best tasting sugary water by the standards of Coca-Cola's own tests. Yet over a century of innovation in marketing, advertising, customer research, licensing and distribution have built what's often spoken of as the most valuable brand in the world.

## *Final Thoughts*

The old cliché is that the only constant is change. Looking around, we can find lots of evidence for that. But the problem with thinking that way is that it can put you in a mindset which is constantly reactive, where you are always on the back foot, responding to events, customers, competitors and the economy.

Let's readjust that cliché: imagine what would happen if you approached your business with the thought that *the only constant is innovation*.

## ENTREPRENEURIAL EMPLOYEES

I've recently worked with Aston University to run an Entrepreneurship Programme for engineering researchers. I was assisted by a number of associates, as well as local entrepreneurs, MDs and professional advisors. When I've mention the programme to my consulting clients, they show great interest – the typical sentiment being: "I wish I could get my employees to be more entrepreneurial – could your programme help us?"

The short answer is yes and no. The entrepreneurship of individuals who start up their own businesses is different to the kind of behaviour that corporates want.

The three factors which must be in place for entrepreneurial (and indeed any other) desirable organizational behaviour are:

1. Clear expectations
2. Skills, tools and know-how (the area the Aston programme focused on)
3. Culture that supports rather than works against the desired behaviour.

The mistake for a large organization would be to try to provide skills training without addressing expectations and culture.

Here's a quick (and – you may decide when you look at the scoring system – somewhat brutal) quiz to help you zero in on factors to address if you want to improve entrepreneurialism within, rather than outside, an organization.

None of these questions should be answered casually. My experience is that the first answer is often wishful thinking and further digging shows that the reverse is really the case.

1. **Is it regarded as normal for people to come up with ideas and seek backing for them?**

Yes ☐  No ☐

2. If and when they do so, do employees suggest credible initiatives?

Yes ☐ No ☐

3. When employees bring you ideas, do they make sense in the context of your mission and strategy?

Yes ☐ No ☐

4. Are initiatives constrained by preset budgets, or is there a willingness to look for money for a good proposition that was previously not envisaged?

Yes ☐ No ☐

5. Can people easily get quick approval and small amounts of time and money to try things out?

Yes ☐ No ☐

6. Do you praise and support well thought out, bold ideas, whether they succeed or fail?

Yes ☐ No ☐

7. Do employees have systematic ways to consider risk-reward trade-offs when making suggestions?

Yes ☐ No ☐

8. Are people promoted for attempts to make money, or because of their social ingratiation with the right people? (Answer this one by looking at actual promotion decisions – it's easy to be led astray with wishful thinking.)

Yes ☐ No ☐

9. **Is the emphasis in your organization on finding better ways to do things (rather than making sure that it's "business as usual" / a peaceful life)?**

Yes ☐ No ☐

10. **Can you easily identify employee-initiated ideas which have resulted in substantial contributions to overall organizational performance?**

Yes ☐ No ☐

## Scoring

**10-9 Yeses**. This sounds like a very entrepreneurial organization and you almost certainly scan for further ideas and opportunities constantly.

**8-7 Yeses**. There is likely scope for substantial gains, as you have many elements in place. The items you responded "No" to are worth bringing to your next senior team meeting or away day.

**6-0 Yeses**. Your culture doesn't seem to support entrepreneurial behaviour, and change is likely to require strong leadership from someone prepared to take on those benefiting from the status quo (on the bright side: you can save money on training – there's no point while the culture doesn't support the desired behaviours when they get back from the workshop).

# CHAPTER EIGHT

# DRIVING STRATEGIC PRIORITIES

At some point, almost every client I have ever consulted with has wanted to mull over the following question: "Of all the things we could be doing, which should we be doing?"

The question comes in many versions:

- Which of our current operations should we continue or discontinue?

- Which opportunities should we pursue or ignore?

- Which projects should we start, continue to back, turn down, or stop?

Alternatively, there's a more general sense of frustration, often expressed as follows:

- "It takes forever for the team to make a strategic decision."

- "We seem finally to agree, but then it all gets opened up again at the next meeting."

- "We agree, but then everyone goes off and does something different anyway."

And on other occasions, the question comes wrapped in a Product-Market ("Ansoff") Matrix which, rather than clarifying things, ends up just rewording the question into: "Should we pursue these new products or these new markets, or both, or...?"

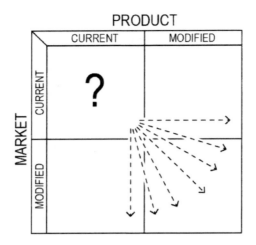

Figure 8.1: Which direction will you grow in?

It's easy to get bogged down – especially when faced with a greater number of appealing options than you can realistically handle.

Many people are tempted to resolve the resulting impasse by collecting more and more data, in the hope that analysis will show the best way forward. But that data is of necessity historical, and so its analysis alone can't decide the overall nature and direction that the business should take. In the end, strategy is a matter of making choices which cannot be entirely reduced to hard data.

The problem these clients are confronting is a strategic one, but the discussion tends to blur into operational terms, and hence get muddy and confused. Strategy involves making high-level commitments which will guide the specific decisions about what to do and also, importantly, what NOT to do. Without that strategic clarity, it's easy to go chasing after every promising idea which pops up, and the results are familiar:

- Insufficient focus to achieve a critical mass in any one area.

- Proliferation of brands which end up competing and confusing the customer.

- Dilution of resources.

- Unnecessary internal competition as people fight for their pet projects.

- Convergence with competitors as the firm and its rivals all try to offer everything, destroying their differentiation in the eyes of buyers.

The following sections provide information that clients have found helpful in order to bring shape to their strategic discussions and to create actionable priorities.

## What's Your Strategic Driving Force?

It's very revealing to think of any business as being shaped primarily by one of nine 'strategic areas': [3]

- the market it serves
- the nature of the products or services it offers
- its production capabilities
- its method of sale
- its method of distribution
- its access to resources
- its technological know-how
- its profit guidelines, or
- its growth aspirations (see table for examples)

In any given business at a particular time, one of these areas will predominate. Clarifying the dominant area – the business's driving force – provides an invaluable

---

[3] This idea was developed by Tregoe and others at the consultancy firm Kepner-Tregoe, and was first introduced to me by Alan Weiss. It is an extremely useful way to provoke focused discussion on the nature and direction of the business.

filter for resolving the confusions I raised at the start of the chapter. The table lists the forces and gives examples of the effect each force has, together with well-know companies that (as far as we can tell without asking their top management) seem to be driven by that force.

Note that all businesses will have vital activities in most if not all of the nine areas. The idea is that one area, for better or worse, shapes decision-making more than the others.

| Driving Force | Typical Path of Growth | Example |
|---|---|---|
| **Market served** | Modified or new products/services to existing, well-understood markets. Asks "What extra, especially higher value, needs can we meet?" | *Saga offer an increasing array of products and services to older people.* |
| **Products/services offered** | Same or modified products or services to new markets (either geographic or demographic). Asks: "Who else will value this?" May also find new uses for existing products. | *Nokia during its period of highest growth.*<br><br>*Arm & Hammer rebranded their baking powder as fridge deodoriser.* |
| **Production capability** | Optimises its current processes and seeks more highly-valued uses for its production capabilities. Seeks projects/contracts which increase utilisation of productive assets. Asks: "What else can we make or provide this way?" | *Commercial printers*<br><br>*Large consultancies* |

| | | |
|---|---|---|
| **Method of sale** | Additional products which can be presented to the buyer using the existing sales process. Asks: "What else can we sell this way? Who else would buy this way?" | *Amazon* |
| **Method of distribution** | Modified or new products which can be brought to market through existing channels. Asks: "What else can we get out to people this way?" | *McDonalds*<br><br>*Tesco (sell in stores and online, but in both cases, distribution is through stores).* |
| **Technology/ Expertise** | Modified or new applications of proprietary technology or expertise. Asks: "Where else would this technology add value?" | *Intel*<br><br>*Honda (in engines)*<br><br>*Autonomy Corporation* |
| **Natural Resource** | Might seek to acquire new sources, transport commodities to new markets. May forward integrate and then adopt an alternative driving force. | *Alcoa*<br><br>*BHP Billiton* |
| **Profit** | Few companies are purely profit driven. Those that are will build or acquire businesses wherever they think there is a best return for their capital. | *Berkshire Hathaway*<br><br>*Hedge Funds* |
| **Growth** | Usually a temporary driving force which is then replaced by another as the business matures. | *Research in Motion (in 2009)* |

Table 8.1: Defining your strategic driving force

As a simple visualisation, here's how a business's emphasis shifts according to whether or not it chooses a market-served or products-offered driving force. Following Tregoe's example, I've extended the original Ansoff game-board to make the transition from box to box more evolutionary – it can be extremely useful to extend this even further by segmenting the markets and product ranges.

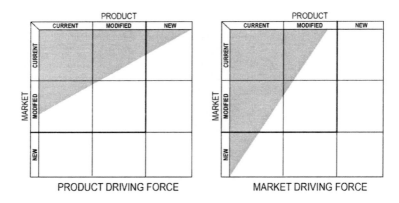

Figure 8.2: How your choice of high-level driving
force shapes the product-service journey

The high-level choice of driving force starts to shape the journey through a product-service matrix. It provides a rational way to avoid the diluted effort of "branching out in all directions", and brings coherence to discussion about strategic choices (for example, decisions about investment in technology, distribution channels, partnering, outsourcing or integration of value chain steps all change as you consider alternative driving forces).

# *Examples*

Here are some examples of how the driving force idea can bring illumination to strategic conversations.

## Whitbread: From brewery to hotels and restaurants

At what we can call stage one in the industry's evolution, breweries historically were driven by a product driving force: they made beer. They quickly evolved to stage two extending further along the value chain into "hospitality", i.e. pubs and hostelries – modifying their driving force but still driven by the products and services offered.

Some brewers then moved to a third driver: for economically appealing reasons they came to think of themselves increasing as property companies. This was even seen as a clever (or fortuitous) hedge against a declining pub market. At one point, a typical buy recommendation for shares in a brewer might note that the asset value of their properties was higher than their market capitalization – managing their property assets created more value than their operations. They increasingly developed freehold property acquisition and management skills and strategic decisions have inevitably been shaped by managers who had developed that orientation. One source at M&B notes the difficulty of his managers considering offering hospitality services on the modern high street where premises are typically leased rather than bought and managed – the de facto driving force has become method of distribution (freehold pubs), or perhaps production capability (utilisable space). Look how inflexible to customer demand this has made them.

However, contrast this with Whitbread. It's a highly successful company that has nothing to do with making beer any more. In order to do that, it had to have confidence and clarity to define itself as driven by the services it offers, not its historical distribution network, and therefore able to consider alternative products and distribution outlets and acquisitions. Whitbread is clear that it is the hospitality business, not the property business.

### Amazon: Which driving force do you think?

What is Amazon's driving force? Try answering it before reading on. I use this question to check whether or not a group of executives have grasped the concept of driving force (for example prior to us using it to think about *their* strategy).

The knee-jerk responses are often either *Products-offered* or *Technology*, but I think we can exclude both of these quite quickly. Amazon started out selling books, for sure, but then it went on to offer CDs, DVDs, then clothes and electrical goods. It continues to offer an even wider range of products, expanding the offerings further through its marketplace arrangements with associate businesses. Unlike Waterstones or Barnes and Noble, Amazon's product-market decisions are not determined by a commitment to a particular type or few types of products.

What about *technology* as a candidate driver then? Amazon is an online business, and it uses clever software, for example to make recommendations to regular customers about books or films they might enjoy. It is certainly in some loosely defined way "a technology company". But if it were a technology *driven* company, its main thrust for growth would be by applying its expertise in areas such as software development and user interfaces to other product/service/market combinations.

Although we would have to talk to its top management to be sure, Amazon actually looks most like a *"method of sale"-driven* company.[4] It sells an

---

[4] Thanks to Alan Weiss for the original insight.

increasingly wide range of things that share the characteristic that can be displayed and delivered within its online shopping environment and where delivery and returns handling can be handled using third party couriers and postal services.

Notice how different Amazon would be if it really was *product* or *technology* driven. Then, and here is the true value of the driving force concept, imagine how diffused its business would be if its managers were incongruently trying to pursue all three drivers at once.

## Could you change if you wanted to?

I've talked elsewhere about the problems Digital had in moving from a technology driving force to a market driver. It's worth a quick mention in this context too. I make the point that Digital's management knew they had to make the shift – they recognised that the market wanted packaged computing "solutions" that they could use without needing to become techies – but   they couldn't fulfil the strategic imperative for cultural reasons: essentially, their engineers liked building ever-more-clever machinery. My guess is that the Digital case is a paradigm for the issues facing many other businesses in many industries as they mature – as emphasis shifts from early adopters to the later majorities, there is less patience among buyers for steep learning curves: they want things that fit into their existing lifestyles with ease and without disruption.

## *Questions To Consider*

For a rich debate which is truly strategic, review the list of driving forces and examples, and then consider the following questions:

• What do you and your team consider your current driving force to be?

• Do you agree with each other?

• What are the operational consequences of any disagreement?

• What other driving forces might make sense for you to consider?

• How would the business look under each alternative? How would priorities change in areas such as resource allocation, investment, project criteria, marketing, and product or service development?

• Is your current driving force the right one for your future, or do you need to move towards a new one?

Once you have reaffirmed or changed your strategic driver, you then need understand how to implement consistently with it. You need to protect current activities while simultaneously putting things into place to support new ones. How do you do that without immediately getting bogged down in too much detail?

## *Final Thoughts*

The Driving Force concept is a penny that can take a while to drop – you have to play with it: applying it to businesses you know, asking yourself how they would change if the driving force changed. Once you get it, it very quickly enables you to improve the quality of strategic conversations. For example, companies which feel they lack strategic clarity, or are finding it hard to translate a strategy into action, can find that they are trying to pursue contradictory driving forces at the same time: for example attempting to maximise utilisation of assets producing lower margin products (which could be appropriate to a production capability driving force) while undermining themselves by chasing market opportunities (consistent with a market need driving force) requiring new assets they can't hope to make profitable unless they reposition as a high-margin business.

Driving forces are worth the effort it takes to understand them, because once you do, the clarity is highly rewarding.

# CHAPTER NINE

# HOW TO BALANCE THE SHORT AND LONG TERM

Jack Welch observed that anyone can run a business for the short term if they don't have to worry about long-term survival, and anyone can strategise if they never have to implement.

The trick is to do both at the same time. A very simple and valuable tool for getting a handle on this short-term-to-long-term tension is the Three Horizons[5]:

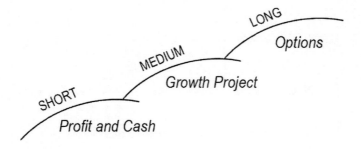

Figure 9.1: The Three Horizons © 1999 McKinsey & Company, Inc.

In essence the Three Horizons framework suggests:

- The short horizon is about profit and cash – it's all about creating operational efficiency, current customer satisfaction etc.
- The medium term horizon is about a committed effort to grow a new business, work stream or client relationship. The emphasis is on the top line. In time, this business should become

---

[5] Formulated by Baghai and colleagues in *The Alchemy of Growth.*

97

established, repay investment, and then take its place as a new short-horizon activity.

- The longer term is where you develop options, exploring possible future growth activities, and sort out the great ideas from the merely good ones with pilot projects and experiments.

It's crucial to realise that you don't wait to finish horizon one before moving on to horizon two or three – in fact *all three require some action now*, and on an ongoing basis. Many firms give much less urgency to the "long" horizon than they should, for example, and leave themselves open to threats from more imaginative competitors.

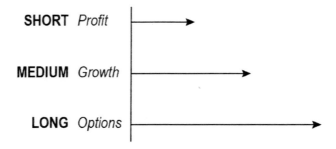

Figure 9.2: All horizons have the same starting point: *today!*

The projects at each horizon form a pipeline which can be managed with discipline to ensure sustainable success over the long-term. In an insightful interview in the CNBC's *The Leaders* series, much-admired Reckitt Benckiser CEO Bart Becht makes it clear how his company systematically creates and commercialises new products in a way which follows exactly this process.

The Three Horizons is a great diagnostic for a business's ability to manage the tension between running the business and building the business. There are eight possible configurations, and the goal is to have a tick at all three levels.

Here are some of the patterns which can occur, along with possible interpretations:

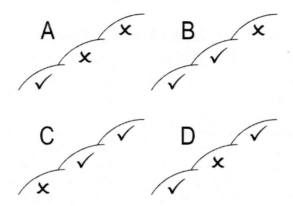

Figure 9.3: Some possible Three Horizon configurations

- **A** is complacent. They may be fine as long as nothing changes – but things change.

- **B** is much better off than A, but *may* be overly committed to one plan or be too trusting that the future environment will continue much like the present.

- **C**, in the language of Baghai and colleagues, is losing the right to grow. They are more excited about the future than the present and are neglecting their existing commitments.

- **D** is competent at their present responsibilities and has great ideas, but fails to bring these ideas into fruition. A classic corporate example is Xerox, who invented all the key elements of the modern PC (windows, mice, pull down menus etc.) but left it to Apple to bring them to market.

Questions to discuss with your team:

- What is the current state of the business at each of the Three Horizons?

- What needs to happen, given our answers?

## *You Can Have Your Cake and Eat it, But Not at The Same Time*

Chapter Eight identifies a key strategic question: "Of all the things we could be doing, which should we be doing?" and we have probably all experienced the problems of trying to pursue too many avenues at once.

A major cause of difficulty is quite simply fear of missing out on a good opportunity, which leads to starting lots of projects. But the big danger – the one that a strategy is supposed to prevent in the first place – is that by trying to do too many things and hedge too many bets, effort is diluted to the point where although you are busy, you don't earn an overall return.

Of course, once people get together in meetings, everyone has their pet ideas about what to take forward; discussion can go around in circles for months. The Three Horizons can be a great device for transforming the deadlock into a constructive discussion. Instead of arguing for X versus Y, it's much more productive to discuss questions such as:

- Should we do this now, or is there something that would be better done first?

- Can we actually build the capability for Y by doing X?

- If we tackle this item on the middle rather than long horizon, do we have enough resource to keep the short, medium and long plates spinning at the same time?

## *Developing and Sequencing Your Strategic Growth Priorities*

Used together, the Product-Market Matrix, Driving Force and Three Horizons provide a neat way to organize your deliberations and communicate a workable sequence for strategically consistent growth to colleagues. An organization with a market-served driver will need to continue to deliver efficiently its current and perhaps modified products to its current market. It may also be introducing and growing the volume of one new product to its current, and perhaps to a modified, market. For longer-term growth options, it may be exploring options involving modifications for both markets and products, and continuing to think about completely new products within its basic market thrust.

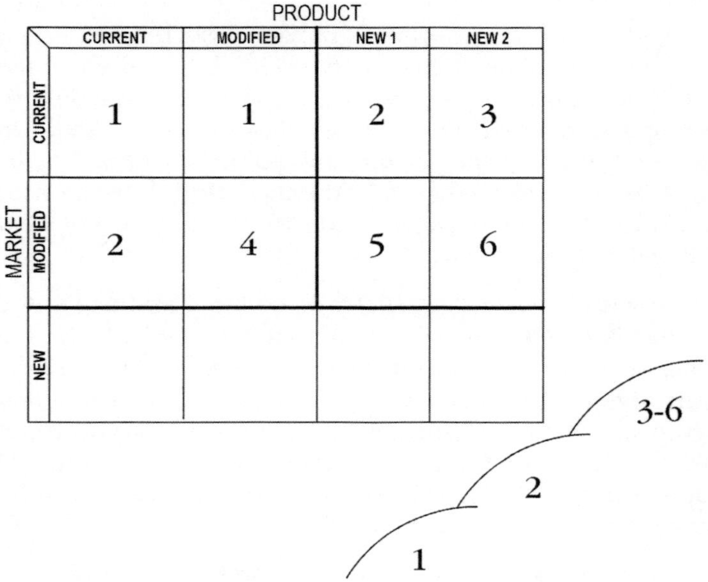

Figure 9.4: Combining Product-Market Matrix, Driving Force and Three Horizons

## *Using a Market Served Driving Force and Three Horizons To Choose and Communicate High-Level Priorities*

Once they have done the hard work of thrashing out their chosen driving force, its implications for product and market segments, and the strategic timing captured by the horizons, it is then actually quite straightforward to link strategic discussions to tangible plans. New proposals can be quickly assessed for both high-level strategic fit and "implementability". Time and frustration are saved, and execution proceeds with renewed focus and urgency.

You can also use this as the basis of the stories you tell your investors and talent.

---

**THE RIGHT RESPONSE TO THE WRONG SITUATION**

Have you ever found yourself trying to put the kettle into the fridge, thinking that you were actually replacing the milk? Perhaps you even noticed the kettle wouldn't fit before you realised why, and so tried to jam the thing in harder? Psychologists call this an "action slip" (the classic book is *The Psychology of Everyday Things* by Donald Norman). Another example would be taking the lid off a can and throwing the can away.

The essence of the action slip is doing the right thing at the wrong time. The mental mechanism that underlies it the same that a fencer, boxer or bowler tries to exploit: training their opponent into a particular response, and then taking advantage of the resulting blind spot to land a successful attack. The loser becomes conditioned to a comfortable pattern and doesn't notice they are trying to apply it in the wrong situation.

Here are some examples of analogous problems in business:

---

- **Relying solely on continuous improvement to the detriment of innovation:** Getting better and better at delivering something while failing to notice that people are getting less and less interested in buying it (e.g. The Digital Equipment Corporation (DEC) made the market-leading VAX minicomputers but didn't adjust to people migrating to networks of cheap desktop PCs).

- **Trying to repeat past successes that are well past their sell by date:** Jaguar based the visual design of the S-type on the classic Mark II, ending up with something that looked nice (if too much like the similarly-inspired Rover 75), but was outclassed in the eyes of many by a dazzling modern Mercedes or BMW. Look how much better the subsequent more contemporarily-styled Jags are doing.

- **Not noticing that one's power base has eroded:** Staff departments such as HR and IT, used to dictating the way the rest of a company deals with them, rigidly repeat bureaucratic procedures until they find themselves being outsourced.

- **Relying on outdated cultural assumptions:** Many in the traditional professions who grew up during the deferential post-WW2 period have been slow to recognise that 21$^{st}$ century clients are neither intimidated nor impressed by status or professional trappings and have no compunction about shopping around and negotiating hard on fees.

The antidote is to remain aware of the changing ends required by customers, and by one's own business, not automatically to favour historically successful means, and make sure you have sensible activities to address the likely future at all three time horizons.

James Dyson's approach is instructive. According to a recent interview on CNBC, his starting point is to go back to people's everyday experiences, discover their repeated frustrations, and then search for answers using both existing capabilities and the capacity of Dyson's engineers to develop new ones.

This is no argument against seeking incremental improvements in efficiency and skill, reductions in slack and inventory, and increases in the automation of existing processes. But at the very least, working backwards from desired results provides a reassuring check that the direction of your continuous improvement is still relevant. And at the most, it can avoid catastrophic failure, or even lead to a decisive breakthrough.

Now if Dyson would just design a kettle that fits in my fridge...

# CHAPTER TEN

# BEWARE OF "STRATEGIC PLANNING"

If you hear someone talking about "Strategic Planning", then question them carefully. They may just be being a bit intellectually lazy; but far worse, they could be betraying a fundamental misunderstanding, because strictly speaking, the term is an oxymoron.

Planning and strategy are, to use my friend Paul Clusker's image, like oil and water in a car engine. You need them both, but don't let them get mixed up.

A plan is simply an orderly sequence of activities designed to achieve a goal. But what determines your goals? If you skip the strategic thinking, your goals will likely be couched in terms of more, or better or bigger amounts of what you have already been doing. They will tend to be about playing the game you are in better, rather than getting into a better game. Here are some of the main problems:

- Plans based on extrapolations from the past tend to keep you going in the same general direction. They don't address the issue of whether that's where you want to go, or need to go.

- Plans based on extrapolation tend to assume that external conditions will remain more or less the same – clearly a dangerous basis on which to proceed. What if the market is drying up? What if new competitors or technological trends are going to make your products obsolete? Norton don't sell many motorbikes any more.

- The level at which longer-term goals are set is determined by current and past limitations. This is one of the problems with the popular idea of

SMART goals, too. The R stands for realistic. Realistic according to what standards? The answer is always going to be in according to the standards of past experience – fine for performance management perhaps, but destined only to be a drag on any serious effort at innovation.

- If they are being honest, most managers will concede that long-range plans are actually a lot more short range than they would like to admit. For example, in most five year plans, it's only the first year that tends to be elaborated in any detail. It's easy to end up just going through the motions when thinking any further ahead.

- Planning by extrapolation is very inward-looking – you run the risk of getting better and better at supplying what your customers are becoming less and less interested in.

## Strategise First, Then Plan Backwards

The goals you plan to achieve are better derived from your strategy for tomorrow rather than by extrapolating your operations of yesterday. Your strategy is the framework which provides the goals – it guides selection of the products, services, markets, sources of competitive advantage, key capabilities and resources you will rely on to create future value.

Once you have your objectives, it's my further recommendation to *plan backwards*. By reversing from the desired future into the present, it's possible to avoid falling foul of past, learned limitations. It has to be said that starting with the future requires considerable mental agility in practice, and many managers who recognise the value of the idea don't do it simply because they just don't have the tools.

Below is a process which I've used successfully with leaders, teams and individual contributors on many occasions. It allows you to suspend assumptions about what's possible long enough to develop actionable plans for achieving big goals. It uses the idea of a time-line – either physically laid out on the floor, or on a table top, flip-chart or white-board as appropriate. I'll explain it as if you are going to walk through it on the floor because many clients find this approach works best.

## A process for Future-to-Present goal setting

Identify and stand on a timeline, starting from the present and looking out into the future.

Pick *a really big,* strategic, worthwhile goal, without, at this stage, being concerned about how realistic it is.

Stand to the side of the timeline and identify a position on the line, and in the future, where "someone" or "some organization" is successfully involved in achieving that compelling, if apparently unreasonable, goal.

Identify the step *just before* "that someone" or "that organization" achieved the goal. Ask the key question:

"What has to *already* be there (or be true) in order for 'that someone' or 'that organization' to achieve the goal as a natural next step?"

Step into that position and check that *if* you were there, you could take the next step and realise the goal.

*Natural Next Step*

The position you've identified now becomes the new (stepping stone) goal.

Now ask yourself, is the stepping stone an unreasonable goal for *you*?

If it is, use the same process again. Make the stepping stone the goal for "someone" (as in Step 3) and identify the step before it (using the key questions from Step 4). Keep going until you reach a "reasonable" stepping stone.

If the stepping stone is reasonable – you're ready to get started.

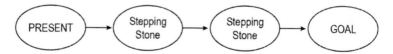

Key Points:

- Strategic questions (What?) are best kept separate from, and addressed prior to, planning questions (How?).
- Goals that bring innovative or dramatic results should be set *without* due regard to the past, at least to start with.
- Planning how to achieve goals is best done backwards, and that is made much easier by having a systematic process such as the one outlined.

## Final Thoughts

One of the most fascinating results of this kind of backward planning is that apparent limitations of the present situation can almost miraculously evaporate. Forward planning often seems like you are pushing a locked door, when actually it simply needs to be pulled. When you reverse through the door from the other side, the door opens easily.

## LESSONS FROM HISTORY FOR TURBULENT TIMES

**This is not the last recession:** A classic mistake in military strategy is to prepare to fight the last war rather than the next one, and the classic example is the Maginot line that the French built between the First and Second World Wars. This line of fortifications along their eastern border assumed that fixed trench warfare would continue to be standard procedure, and it left the French badly wrong footed and unable to manoeuvre when faced with the unprecedented conditions created by the Blitzkrieg.

**Don't pull your head in:** French high command at the start of WW2 was holed up in the Château de Vincennes, with very poor communication with the front. In fact, it was described by one observer as like a "submarine without a periscope". See "Stating the (Elusive) Obvious" on page 28 for more on the dangers of detached senior management.

**Self-fulfilling prophecies have a habit of coming true:** In private, Churchill was extremely doubtful about British chances in the early part of the war. In public of course, he projected his legendary determination, and who can doubt it was a galvanising contribution to ultimate success?

**Resist the temptation to spin:** Note that while Churchill was positive, he was also honest. "I have nothing to offer but blood, toil, tears and sweat" is not an appealing sales pitch, but it is straight, and therefore retains credibility. I have done a fair number of focus groups in my time and, believe me, employees and customers see through spin; all it does is weaken confidence and strengthen cynicism. Investors are equally sensitive: imagine a bank saying "there will be no credit losses on our massive portfolio of asset backed securities, because it is of such high quality". Is there a surer way to trigger an immediate sell-off of the bank's shares?

**As Corporal Jones from *Dad's Army* would say: "Don't panic!"** One example of panic is to make across-the-board cuts regardless of difference in performance across the business, or regardless of the hard-to-recover skills and assets that are being discarded. I've been impressed by those of my clients who responded to the economic crisis by taking an intelligent approach to redeploying resources, for example being flexible in moving them from areas where they can't make money to areas where they can, often counter-cyclical ones which currently offer good opportunities.

**Allies make a big difference:** Get to know your customers better. Do they have new needs you could address? Can you help them to cope? Can you spend more time now on those "important but not urgent" relationship-building activities? Can you form alliances with people who are in counter-cyclical businesses and as a consequence have capacity problems?

Finally, in the words of one of my favourite strategists, Colonel John Boyd:

**People, Ideas, Hardware – in that order:** The most tooled-up army doesn't always win, and the biggest marketing budget doesn't always carry the day. Consider that restricted access to capital and other resources can be the mother of invention. I always like the image of Barnes-Wallis developing the idea for the bouncing bomb in his bird pond. In modern business terms: "Talent/Relationships, Viable Strategy, Systems/Processes" – in that order.

## CULTURE AND THE ABILITY TO DELIVER

Culture shapes behaviour, and behaviour influences results. What then creates culture? One thing is clear from many of the focus groups and interviews that I have conducted at varied organizations: much corporate internal communication has either no effect, or a counter-productive one. Younger people in particular have been effectively trained by modern media techniques to interpret anything which sounds too slick as spin. What's more, they have often been socialised by a media that is at best ambivalent about business.

And what are they to do? They want to 'get on', and to be able to enjoy as consumers the products, services and experiences which businesses provide, yet they are suspicious of corporations (and the plentiful supply of corporate BS), may have mixed feelings about being ambitious, competitive and successful (certainly in the UK), and feel vaguely guilty about their carbon footprints.

The prevailing wider culture does not shape behaviour in business-friendly ways – so your organization is going to need to do it. But if you try to manipulate people with facile internal "comms", they will switch off.

It's always worth remembering that the verb "to train" comes from a root meaning "to drag behind". The verb "to educate", of course, comes from a root meaning "to draw out". Leaders need to educate their people to understand the benefits of aligning their own actions with those of the organization. And to avoid being cast as cynical manipulators, that means leading from the front.

(And that means that leaders sometimes have to deal with their own conflicts about the goodness of commercial endeavours, but that is for another time.)

# CHAPTER ELEVEN

# CULTURE SHOCK

A staggering 97% of mergers by UK companies fail to completely fulfil their strategic objectives, according to the Hay Group. Managers who responded to their survey regarded "culture shock" as the main reason for failure.

Typically, the term "culture" is left undefined, and maybe blaming culture when things fail – which is easy to do – lets assorted managers and advisors off the hook. So let's start by asking: if culture is so important to managers, what do they mean by it?

## *What is "Culture" Anyway?*

To many finance and operations officers, "culture" is a woolly concept, while academics and many consultants have done little to clarify the term.

Think of culture simply as *"the beliefs and values that influence behaviour"* in an organization: or in plain words it's "the way we do things round here" and "why we do it this way".

There's no doubt that the wrong culture can kill a company, even a once-formidable global competitor. Ed Schein, arguably the leading authority on corporate culture, has written extensively about the Digital Equipment Corporation (DEC). Over thirty years, starting from 1957, founder and CEO Ken Olsen built DEC to be the world's second largest computer manufacturer after IBM. When I was a university student in software engineering in the 1980s, DEC VAX minicomputers were the leading edge. DEC was an engineering and innovation-based culture where the engineers were the heroes. It had a technology driving force. Its answer to any marketing issue was to build another, even more sophisticated (and costly) piece of kit. And it worked – until the advent of the PC.

When computer hardware became a commodity, DEC knew that they had to develop a market-need driven strategy. They knew it, *but they just didn't want to do it.* It would mean firing senior executives who couldn't change. It would mean saying "no" to engineers with new ideas. It would mean emphasising customer research, service and software applications, rather than ever more glorious technology.

So now, DEC is no more. Xerox (at least in computing) and Wang Labs didn't make the change either.

## How Culture Affects the Nuts and Bolts

Many clients are uneasy about "the soft stuff". It is helpful to focus on the fact that, except in a completely automated business, *executing a business strategy depends on people performing the right behaviours.*

In DEC's case, the behaviours required in the changed world of the 1980s (e.g. designing features based on customer research, and advertising based on customer problem-solving rather than pure technical advance) were not consistent with its values (technological progress for its own sake, engineering as fun, being a senior engineer as a source of pride, engineering as superior to business).

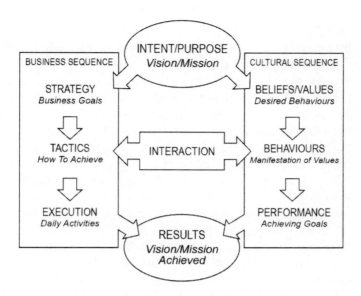

Figure 11.1: The Dynamics of Strategy Implementation
(adapted from Alan Weiss, Process Visual)

Once you think of the culture as simply the governor of the behaviours required by strategy, then, as Alan Weiss's diagram in Figure 11.1 shows, it becomes clear that there are not one but *two* interrelated paths that must be followed to implement successfully: yes, you need to develop strategic objectives, associated tactics and activities, but you also need to make sure that the culture will support people actually doing the behaviours your plans require. Too many managers consider the business sequence alone, with disappointing results played out every day.

## *Culture Clashes Post-merger*

Here's a scenario where an acquirer took on a business which, culturally, it could not run effectively.

Company A, the acquirer, was young, entrepreneurial, fast-growing, innovative and provided a high level of service. For this, it commanded high prices and high margins which enabled it to get away with being disorganized and wasteful in operations. It then took over a less exciting, lower margin, more commodity-oriented business, Company B. This is when disaster struck: a lack of emphasis from Company A managers on execution led to a breakdown of order fulfilment, orders being automatically stopped because of alleged credit problems, a large proportion of the year-end receivables being written off because there were no records of who had and hadn't paid, an inability to fulfil orders because, despite there being sufficient stock for five months' worth of sales in the warehouse, nobody could find it when they needed it...

In short, Company A's beliefs and values – much like DEC's – fought against the disciplined if boring behaviours required to run Company B's processes.

In one high-profile merger which must remain anonymous, the converse to the above situation has taken place. A commodity-oriented manufacturing business, with a near monopoly in its core area, has taken over a higher-end manufacturer in the same broad sector. The target's products include large amounts of customised electronics and its people are used to a high level of cooperation with customers. The acquirer has, however, imposed a heavily siloed structure on its acquisition to prevent clients easily negotiating cost reductions (they now have to deal with five or six reps rather than one). This is a hardball mentality which works well with the core, near-monopoly business, but is at odds with the partnership ethos of the acquisition. It remains to be seen what the effect is, but reps with candid relationships with clients are getting "forthright" feedback, and customers are not without alternative suppliers.

## Six Tactics for Transition Management

Just as "mergers and acquisitions" or "M&A" subsumes a range of transactions, so it gives rise to a variety of post-deal management situations. The appropriate mix of tactics will also vary accordingly: here are six of the most broadly applicable. These tactics apply just as well in culture change initiatives that are not simply the result of post-deal integration (for example as a result of a clear change in strategy).

### 1. Think about behaviours required to execute the new strategy

Look at the situation through the lens provided by the Strategy Implementation sequences in Figure 11.1. For a business model to be executed, and for customers to have the required experiences at the right times, certain behaviours are logically implied. In order for those behaviours to occur, they, and their consequences, must be highly prioritised and valued by the culture. At a minimum you will see what has to be changed; at a maximum you may rethink the deal altogether.

For example, in the transition from a technology-driven strategy (such as DEC's) to a marketing-led strategy, priorities, behavior and incentives have to change significantly.

### 2. Assess what is changing for people – tackle negative effects

A new management team may face a number of changes which could negatively affect performance:

- The team may be accustomed to using many support services from a corporate centre which they will no longer be able to access: HR, IT,

Learning & Development, Legal, Finance. Often they won't notice what they are missing until they have an urgent need for it.

- They may have had an extremely hands-on former owner, CEO or MD, meaning that while they have been individually competent, they have never *really* been a team – the boss did the coordinating and decision-making.

- Alternatively, they may have "grown up" being very cooperative, but have insufficient definition of roles for the new organization to grow.

- They may be competent managing in a stable state, cushioned by a larger entity, but lack experience of managing for aggressive growth driven by high levels of debt.

- They may poorly handle the staff's inevitable feeling of uncertainty, leading to rumours and the avoidable loss of important managers (the best ones find it easiest to move), reduced morale, poor customer service and increased staff turnover.

Any one of these can ruin a merger, and more than one at a time is not uncommon. Look over your list. What problems may arise? How can they be prevented? What contingency plans can you establish in case they occur?

### 3. Make change more comfortable

If you say "Change or die", many people will respond by sticking their head in the sand and carrying on doing what they've always done. They've made the Smoking Kills warning on the cigarette packets bigger than the top line at the opticians – but cigarettes are still flying off the shelves.

So attempting to frighten people into changing is counter-productive. But people can and do change when they see it as advantageous and tolerable to do so. Look at all those formerly computer-phobic pensioners who now can't imagine life without texting or the Skype.

The trick is to reduce the fear-inducing uncertainty created by the 'ambiguous zone' through which people must travel in order to arrive at where they need to be.

This is where a leader's storytelling skills are at a premium. Paint a verbal picture of an "intermediate scenario". Many leaders communicate their ultimate vision quite well, but less of them communicate what it will be like on the way. Make that zone less ambiguous and threatening by communicating not only the final objective and its benefits, but also what to expect while the change is happening: if you can't make it comfortable, at least make it "do-able".

## 4. Go and meet people

Amazing but true: people buy companies and don't meet the people for weeks or months. This is the most effective way to fuel a rumour mill. And while people are focused on the rumours, they are not focusing on customers. The meeting process doesn't have to be in the form of official presentations (in fact these are unlikely to be believed most of the time).

Some ideas:

- Avoid coming over like a visiting dignitary
- Leave the PowerPoint behind
- Have lunch in the staff cafeteria

Remember that, overall, actions speak louder than words.

### 5. Meet the key influencers early

In any organization there will be certain opinion leaders who others look to for guidance. But these are often not the "official" bosses.

Remember the two marines charged with murder in the film *A Few Good Men*? One is the charismatic and purposeful Lance Corporal Dawson, and the other is Private First Class Downey, who is naïve and has some learning difficulties. He is described as "idolising" the Lance Corporal. Whenever something in the court proceedings occurs that he doesn't understand, or that frightens him, the Private turns to Dawson (not the judge or even his own defence team although they are all officers) as the source he trusts in order to find out what is going on and what to do about it.

The way to change organizational culture is to find and influence the influencers. To influence Private Downey, you have to win over Lance Corporal Dawson. Similarly, if a respected supervisor thinks you are ok, you will get the support of everyone who looks up to him or her.

### 6. Coach key individuals

Most managers have not had the opportunities to develop their technical and people skills equally. An external coach can bring objective questioning, a sounding board, and a deeper knowledge of communication and change to bear during the crucial transition period.

One client acquired a call-centre operation and asked us to work with the newly-appointed General Manager. The Manager had been with the company since its inception around a decade earlier and had been promoted "from the ranks". He was now required to deliver against much more stretching targets than before the acquisition. The challenge for the manager was to assert authority and control without damaging the morale of the staff. We helped him work out conflicts with former peers who are now his direct reports, and with a former boss who is now his peer. Getting past these issues freed up his time to deal with the challenges of delivering results in a much higher performance environment.

## *Final Thoughts*

In summary, the six tactics for smooth transition management are:

1.  Think about behaviours required to execute the new strategy

2.  Assess what is changing for people – are there negative effects which can be headed off or mitigated?

3.  Make change more comfortable, rather than making staying the same more frightening

4.  Go and meet people informally

5.  Find out who the key influencers are, and meet them early

6.  Coach key individuals

None of these are expensive. In fact, numbers 4 and 5 cost almost nothing, but that doesn't mean we should underestimate their value. We tend to equate *effort in* with *effort out:* if something is easy (especially if it is soft and intangible), we don't see that it could have a big return. Just these two actions can quieten the rumour mill, give you leverage in influencing the culture in your favour, and make the merger more successful.

**HAVE YOU NOTICED HOW SIMILAR STRATEGY REVIEWS ARE TO NEW YEARS' RESOLUTIONS?**

How many times have you held off-site meetings, documented a shiny new strategy, launched it – and then everyone has carried on doing the same old things?

It frustrates managers, and it frustrates their teams too. In fact when I talk with staff in all kinds of businesses, I often hear at some point: "We've had so many new initiatives launched that run out of steam – this is just another one – nothing will actually change."

**The force field that defeats willpower**

Resolutions are up against a powerful force: people are creatures of habit. And because organizations are made up of people, organizations are creatures of habit too.

The force of habit shapes behaviour like a magnetic field organizes a pattern of iron filings. If you try to move the filings without realigning the force field, the filings get pulled back automatically.

What determines the shape of the organizational "force field"? There are a number of factors which can be uncovered by a systematic diagnosis, but particularly powerful – and often overlooked – are *unintended consequences,* e.g.:

- It's more rewarding to do the old thing. For example: the new strategy might call for an emphasis on an updated service to unfamiliar clients, but people stick to order-taking for old products with clients they know well, get better short term numbers, then get a bigger bonus than someone who tried to do the right thing.

- The change takes more time and effort, but goes unrecognised, so people think, "Why bother? It's extra work for nothing." As one manager said to me recently "Around here, praise is the absence of criticism" – not very motivating.

- The changed behaviour involves risk, and, whatever managers may say, people just don't believe they can make mistakes without suffering consequences. For example: I've come across railway bosses who say they want people to treat safety as the highest priority, then whack them for causing delays – naturally the employees take time-saving short-cuts if they think they can get away with it. Read some transport accident reports, or look into the recent history of BP operations in Texas and the Gulf of Mexico – this happens a lot.

**Look at the workplace as your people see it**

To figure out why resolutions on behalf of employees go awry, and get clues as to what to do about it, put yourself in their shoes, and ask the following questions:

- What *really* happens to me if I try to put the new action into practice?
- What is the immediate consequence?
- What are the knock-on consequences? For me? For others?
- What's really in it for me?
- What are the risks? Are they worth the potential benefit?

Then return to your own shoes, and ask:

- What do we have to do to ensure that the magnetic field is working *for* us, and there are no unintended consequences constantly pulling people back to the old ways?

# CHAPTER TWELVE

# FIVE THEMES FOR HIGH PERFORMING LEADERSHIP TEAMS

The way senior teams work together has a huge influence on results. The stakes can be very high because rational resource allocation, cross-functional coordination and timely decision-making all depend on leadership team dynamics. If you want to boost team performance, here are five good areas to consider:

| Theme | Problems show up as... | Benefits of getting it right... |
|---|---|---|
| Is it really a team, or just a committee? | *Turf wars, politics, silo behaviour, lack of action, chronically slow decision cycles* | *The whole becomes greater than the sum of its parts* |
| Are people aware of different decision making and communication patterns? | *Unnecessary friction, misunderstandings and "personality clashes"* | *Effective collaboration, reduced errors, reduced conflict* |
| Are the goals big enough? | *Lack of inspiration, going through the motions* | *Energy, enthusiasm, challenge* |
| Is there clear role separation? | *Too many requests to the leader to sort out turf wars, lots of time wasted spinning wheels* | *Cooperation and coordination, individuals feel they are making a clear contribution* |
| Does the team use best practice for meeting productivity? | *Boring unsatisfying meetings, lack of follow-through on agreed actions, unwillingness to attend* | *Best use of skills and talents of members, increased project speed, better decisions, clearer accountability* |

Table 12.1: Five areas of consideration for boosting team performance

The following sections look at each area in turn.

## *Have You Actually Got a Team, or is it Just a Committee?*

A lot of so-called teams are actually committees made up of independent parties with individual agendas. Their meetings are arenas for wasteful zero-sum games (politics, turf wars etc.). Below are some questions to test whether you have a team or a committee:

- Is each member's main responsibility and accountability for the group as a whole, or for the performance of his or her own unit?

- Are people clear why they are meeting and what they are supposed to be doing together?

- Is the team too large for people to get good at coordinating with each other? The research suggests that more than six or seven is the danger limit.

- Do substitutes often attend in place of team members, causing a lack of cohesion and continuity?

Sometimes, subconsciously, the leader prefers a committee, because they believe that running the organization is their job alone, and don't want the team to make important decisions at all. However, they rarely find this satisfactory and usually end up exhausted and frustrated with the lack of shared responsibility.

Key Points:

- How can you arrange things so that the group win or lose together: they all share in the rewards of success etc.?

- Can you design your teams to keep the numbers to around six or seven?

- If you are the leader and fear losing control to the team, learn about leadership frameworks such as Vroom and Yetton's (see Chapter Eighteen) that allow you adjust control and delegation to the circumstances.

Finally, don't waste time testing for Belbin[6] team roles if everyone hates each other's guts. If you *do* need a team and people hate each other, you're best hope is probably in changing the membership.

## *Avoiding Communication Traps*

Be aware of your own and other peoples' decision making and communication patterns.

A lot of time is wasted going round in circles that look like fundamental personality clashes, whereas actually they are just mismatches of communication style. In one aircraft component manufacturer, managers and engineers were at loggerheads and constantly obstructed each other, even though they shared the same vital interest in the company's success. The engineers claimed to be the guardians of safety, the managers the champions of viability: they ended up producing an unsafe product and nearly going out of business! They were all pleasant and rational enough to deal with on their own, but when they got together their different communication and thinking styles,

---

[6] Belbin® Team Roles is a popular set of generalisations intended to increase understanding of members' typical contributions to team performance.

conditioned by their different education and training, conspired to produce clashes and errors.

Two major differences to watch for are how people prefer to collect information and how they prefer to make to decisions. For example, the FD may want nitty-gritty details, while the marketing director is talking big picture, which frustrates the FD. In-house legal counsel may be quick to point out problems with a plan, not to rain on anyone's parade, but because it is their pattern to spot what could go wrong. Spotting risks is a pattern that is essential for a lawyer, but it can interrupt the flow of idea generation when looking for alternative courses of action

Surprisingly big changes in team functioning can be brought about just by changing the sequence of contributions. For example, you might let the marketing director generate an idea, have the operations or engineering director flesh it out into something concrete, and then do the risk assessment (often a neglected area in decision making) by letting the FD and in-house counsel look for potential downsides.

More generally, increased awareness of one's own and others' thinking and communication styles and perspectives can greatly increase the quality of results from team meetings, and make the process much more enjoyable and energising.

Key Points:

- What are you doing to further develop your own self-awareness and to adapt to other communication and thinking styles?

- Who are your key stakeholders? What are their styles, and their perceptions? We have to start with the intention to build functioning relationships with everyone on our team, and with our key stakeholders, if we want to expedite business results.

## *Really Big Goals Are Easier To Achieve Than "Realistic" Ones*

"Realistic" goals are based on current perceptions about what's possible. Those perceptions are very often plain wrong – i.e. not realistic at all. And even when they are effective, SMART goals and things of that ilk are usually pretty modest, boring and uninspiring. Goals should get people excited. The response you are after is, "What!? We can't do that! But wouldn't it be great if we could. Hang on, there might be a way." People on a high performance team want to be part of a vision that is compelling, inspiring, and maybe a bit scary.

In coming up with a vision unencumbered by assumptions past their sell-by date, it's vital not to extrapolate from the present. Instead start from the future.

Wonder about the following: "Imagine you work to produce a vision and strategy which you then implement. You turn out to be highly successful. A journalist comes in to see you in three years and you tell them all about it. What do you show them and tell them about while you are giving them the tour? What accomplishments and milestones are you most proud of? What were some of your key challenges? What's next?"

Key Point:

- What are you doing to "raise the bar" on your team's vision? What's the story? Many teams are successful in delivering short-term results, but high performance teams have a compelling, somewhat scary, vision that everyone on the team can get inspired by. Sometimes the thing to do with comfort zones is to leap so far outside them that the old objections to taking action don't make sense any more.

## Clear Role Separation

*"Tie two birds together, and although they have four wings, still they cannot fly."*

Lack of a clear role is a huge obstacle to individual and team performance. It leads to people constantly getting in each other's way instead of focusing on delivering results. Each role needs to be clearly aligned with key objectives so as to help focus individuals and to help set priorities. And this information needs to be shared with everyone on the team to foster collaboration, minimise conflict, and prevent "silo behaviour". People get possessive about yielding responsibilities to new colleagues, and it is tempting to fudge the issue by asking the old and new person to "collaborate". This just doesn't work when the nature of the responsibility means it is best managed by one person. Without clarity, you will find out all about the wisdom of the old Kung Fu movie quote I used to introduce this section.

Key Point:

- Who is accountable for role clarity and key results? The longer you wait to define these, the more people get stressed about "putting in time" versus delivering key results.

## Team Meeting Productivity

Meetings are time- and energy-eating monsters.

When running team meetings and retreats, the first question should be: "How will you know that the meeting has been of value; what will be the specific evidence?" In the absence of this kind of focus, most meeting concentrate not on results but on activities (agenda items, information that should have been shared before the meeting, mind-numbing PowerPoint slides) or politics. High performance teams manage meetings well by ensuring that nothing gets onto the agenda unless it is tied to key results, and that most information sharing is done prior to the meeting. They also establish mechanisms to prevent side-tracking, political point scoring and other discussion irrelevant to the goals of the day.

Key Point:

* What evidence would you offer to convince an outside party that a particular meeting had been valuable? Focus on improving your team's information sharing, problem-solving, and decision-making abilities to expedite team results.

## Final Thoughts

The value of teams has become an article of corporate faith, but actually you can't always have a team, and you don't always need one. Some amount of internal competition is inevitable, and may even be desirable as a spur to high performance. Teams are great and continue to be the best form for many joint tasks, but rather than pretending to be a team when they never can be, ask yourself if it's better for your group to be explicit about fault-lines and have an open, if tough, negotiation.

## ARE YOUR PEOPLE WILLING TO PASS THE BALL?

When we were kids playing football, there was always one guy who would never pass the ball, but instead would try to run the full length of the field and score all on his own. Almost invariably he'd hold on to the ball too long and be tackled, conceding possession to the other side. Even when he did score, the rest of us on his side wouldn't be particularly thrilled, since he seemed more concerned about competing with us for glory than beating our opponents.

Our sports teacher would tell him, "You need to learn to become a team player." This has become a cliché (and the trouble with such clichés is that people nod when they hear them but don't actually think about what they mean). What *does* it really mean to be a team player? I think a lot of it comes down to a willingness to pass the ball.

Why did that kid hang on to the ball? I don't suppose he had insight into his motives, but I'm willing to bet that he enjoyed the feeling of control. And the possibility of personal glory appealed more to him than the risk of losing the game.

In any team sport involving passing and tackling, as a young player matures they change their understanding of what it means to pass. Rather than it meaning "I'm losing control", it becomes something like "We're building something". Rather than it meaning "I can't handle this on my own" (accompanied by a sense of personal weakness), it becomes "I'm calling on the support of my team-mates" (a sign of maturity and effectiveness).

An intermediate stage of progress is passing the ball, but only in desperation! At this point it's usually too late for team-mates to save the situation. In a truly artistic team, players hold on to the ball neither for too long nor too short a time.

I think it's clear how this relates to work-teams. As Alan Weiss points out, most so-called teams in business are actually no such thing. They are just committees. The essential difference between the two is that a team wins or loses together, while the members of a committee can win independently of each other (in fact one member can actually win at the *expense* of another).

So here are three questions to consider in order to foster true team-work:

- Are people on your 'teams' willing to pass the ball (i.e. resources such as people, money, contacts) for the good of the others in the group?

- Do they perceive doing so as being for, or against, their personal interests (and how accurate are their perceptions)?

- Do they act as custodians of the group's resources, neither holding on too long nor passing responsibility on too quickly?

# CHAPTER THIRTEEN

# ARE VIRTUAL TEAMS BETTER THAN "REAL" ONES?

Virtual teams may become the basic unit of future organizations – certainly they are becoming more, not less, important. There appear to be some huge benefits:

- **Massive savings of travel time and costs:** Not only is international travel increasingly inconvenient and fraught, so is domestic travel in many places (a recent survey by the Institution of Civil Engineers estimated that traffic gridlock cost UK businesses £20 billion a year in lost productivity).

- **Increased organization-wide access to talent:** People with particular skills, knowledge and experience can make judicious contributions to many more projects when they don't have to move their location.

- **A new contract between organizations and contributors:** As organizations become increasingly fluid – put together like movie crews on a project-by-project basis – freelancers and consultants can plug in and out of an endeavour easily. And because they have to act as autonomous agents, it frees the centre from many of the costs of being an employer, while encouraging individuals to be more accountable for their contributions.

There is also a spurious driver of virtual teams, which is that they are used "because we can" – because the technology is seductive. But once the gimmick wears thin, is there any reason why a simulated meeting will be any more productive than a real one, just because it is simulated?

If the case for virtual teams is already made, and if we make allowance for the temptations of technology-for-its-own-sake, here are four issues that become pertinent:

1. Real or virtual? It's about fitness for purpose, not just where the members are physically located today.
2. Are there times when a virtual team is better even when you don't need to organize that way?
3. Is there an opportunity to re-think teams altogether?
4. How do you create high performance?

The following sections look at each issue in turn.

## Real or Virtual?

It's about fitness for purpose, not just where the members are physically located today.

British Airways ran an ad campaign in the early 2000s to head off competition from the internet. As it was designed to do, it struck a chord with many people involved in complex sales. It showed a British media executive in his shirt sleeves checking that a prospect in New York had received the full colour designs he had emailed across. The prospect was saying, "Yes we've got it, it looks great", and the media guy was grinning at his staff and giving them a thumbs-up. Then the camera returned to Manhattan to show that as soon as the prospect put the phone down, he turned and warmly extended his hand to greet the competing team (all in immaculate suits), also British, who had flown in for a meeting in person.

Sometimes real is better, and sometimes virtual is better. It's not a matter of a single right answer. What makes the difference? The table is a quick and partial comparison of real, hybrid and pure virtual teams.

| Real teams | Hybrid teams | "Pure" Virtual teams |
|---|---|---|
| Meet face to face on a regular basis | Core is a real team and they are regularly joined by virtual members | Rarely if ever meet face-to-face |
| Good for exchange of tacit knowledge | Need to keep virtual members in the loop | Technology and pure necessity tend to encourage exchange of explicit knowledge |
| More potential manoeuvring/ relationship issues | Virtual members can feel marginalised relative to core members | May be less political/more task oriented |

Table 13.1: A comparison of team types

A key feature of virtual team communication is that it is less analogue and more digital. This has benefits and drawbacks. Analogue communication (which can take place through voice tone, facial expression, physical movement, seating positions, side conversations in breaks) is invaluable when:

- You need to build trust.

- Implicit communication is an important part of team performance – real-time teams such as surgical teams, live TV editors and producers, teams controlling complex systems such as power stations, aircraft etc.

- Emotional tone is a factor that has to be taken into account for consensus building, negotiating and group creativity.

- You want to give people a sense of belonging, loyalty and affiliation.

I have a friend who is a professional session singer who has contributed backing vocals to some very famous hits. She is exquisitely tuned-in to voice inflections, and she knows my speech patterns. Once she phoned me and on hearing me answer (I believe I said, "Hello"). She replied, "You have someone with you, I'll call you later."

Most people can't make that kind of distinction on the phone. In circumstances where nuance and emotional tone are important, not travelling might turn out to be a false economy, and you should all really get on a plane, or physically relocate people.

## Are There Times When a Virtual Team is Better Even When You Don't Need To Organize That Way?

You may miss out on some of the communication nuances, but here are some ways virtual team can be better than real ones, even if the people are on the same physical site:

- **Increased task-orientation:** Although they may be warm and sociable when they want to, most really effective executives waste little time with off-task communication while at work. Being able to switch off the need for social reinforcement (as opposed to task-oriented cooperation) is a differentiator of high performers. Digital communication can encourage higher productivity precisely because there is less opportunity for socialising. Virtual teams do tend to be more task-oriented.

- **Potential for better structure and productivity:** Time-keeping, agendas, minutes, action points are ensured for "free" by the software tools.

- **Less side-tracking:** Face-to-face meetings are often huge timewasters that go in circles and degenerate quickly into forums for political operating (this is when the potential for implicit communication becomes negative – innuendo, hints and mixed messages thrive on analogue communication). In order to contribute to a virtual meeting, you have to be organized and it's harder to cover a lack of preparation with waffle.

- **Creation of explicit history/audit trails:** Here, the built-in tools in the technology provide great convenience for technical teams (programming, drug manufacturing, legal) where a clear, correct explicit audit trail is valuable.

- **Avoidance of groupthink:** We have known for many years about the dysfunctional group dynamics that occur when the situation is emotionally charged and interpersonal influence can bias groups away from making the wisest choices. Virtual communication may actually help to ensure a better, more rational, group process.

- **Reduced emotion in overly charged situations:** In negotiating the Camp David agreement between Israel and Egypt, facilitators shuttled a document between the parties who were located separately. The focus became the document, rather than interpersonal dynamics – the implementation was low-tech, but the principle still applies.

## Is There An Opportunity To Re-Think Teams Altogether?

When I learned computer systems analysis in the early 1980s, the first thing I was taught was that we shouldn't just automate the existing system (that doesn't mean it's not what happens even today, however!). When you fall into that tempting trap, you perpetuate limiting assumptions about the way things should be done, i.e. the way they've always been done.

One way of developing virtual teams it to use technology in order to make the meeting itself as real as possible. Holographic technology now exists that can enable a presenter to appear real to an audience – some was débuted at recent MTV awards. So there will be a holographic WebEx before too long.

Such technology may prove be excellent for negotiations, facilitated meetings and so on where it will lend the non-verbal richness of face-to-face interaction. But will it add to the coordination of team-based projects? Most real team meetings are a dreadful waste of time – why use the wonders of the internet and holography to recreate the effect in cyberspace?

However, the fast-but-not-real-time communication offered by email, text, forums, chat rooms and so on affords some genuinely new ways of increasing productivity, not only through reduced travel time, but through completely new patterns of cooperation and coordination.

Forums in particular offer huge productivity gains. Not only are meetings in virtual space, they are also in virtual time. Some of the benefits:

- You don't lose time in blocks

- You can review people's contributions, and produce *considered* responses

- It's harder for people to waste time politicking and point-scoring

- You can check facts before responding, leading to increased accuracy

- You don't get forced to make expedient decisions under artificially short deadlines

A lot of the advice around working with virtual teams is about creating the shared experiences and sense of history they are perceived to lack. Actually that perceived history might not always be a good thing: a lot of "teams" have members who hate each other, going way back. In some situations, on-line forums may actually be better for teams who are physically located in the same building, never mind scattered across the globe!

## Final Thoughts

Whether your teams interact in person or virtually, the default method of organizing will be formal meetings, and the way in which these are conducted will have a dramatic effect on both the quality and quantity of business that gets done. So let's turn our attention to meetings themselves.

# CHAPTER FOURTEEN

# THE DANGERS OF MEETINGS

Internal meetings definitely contribute cost, but their benefit is generally much less clear. It is also the case that the conduct of external meetings with existing and potential customers can have a major effect on profitability. Frustration with meetings does much to promote a culture of cynicism and low morale and, perhaps most worryingly, in this age of ever-increasing scrutiny, the way groups interact can actually produce worse decisions than individuals! This is true regardless of how competent group members are when acting alone, with sometimes disastrous consequences and potentially serious governance implications (think Enron/Andersen, or the UK Corporate Manslaughter and Corporate Homicide Act).

When it comes to meetings, something strange is going on. Almost everyone knows it, but people just keep going along with it. Consider the following three examples:

1. A friend who works as a research manager for one of the most respected and innovative corporations in the world likes to plays a game with a colleague at meetings: they attempt to work random phrases of pseudo-management-speak into their "contributions" (e.g. "We need to find a way to maximise distribution bandwidth on this concept"). A point is awarded if their words are unknowingly accepted as a genuine contribution by the rest of the people present. The game provides an amusement and intellectual challenge that the meeting itself lacks (I should add that my friend is an extremely competent and conscientious employee who regularly gets to the office at 06:30–

two hours earlier than required – presumably to get some work done before she gets called into a meeting).

2.  I once worked in an organization where a game modelled on the scoring system of cricket evolved: runs and wickets were awarded every time an eccentric manager used certain key phrases.

3.  I was on a committee at which decisions were being made which affected the careers of individuals in their absence. I began to notice that when there was a lack of consensus in the group, the Chair was tending to impose the decision according to the position I had taken. He would propose the decision, and look at me. If I gave a slight nod of agreement, the decision went through. Very uncomfortable for me – and impossible to comment on at the time. I handled it by giving the individuals concerned the benefit of any doubt in every case. By the way, among the members of the committee were published experts in non-verbal communication and group decision making: they were apparently oblivious to what was going on.

## *The Real Costs of Meetings*

In every kind of organization, meetings are generally considered inefficient at best. Meeting organizers often just don't know how to plan and run one. Participants often give meetings low priority and so arrive late, nip out for "quick" telephone calls, split their attention between BlackBerrys and items they consider of low interest, or leave early. Remember this is contributing directly to cost, but not to anything much else.

Furthermore, money is just one part of the cost. Discouraging meetings negatively affect attitudes and morale. They can make people so frustrated that it can take time to become productive and focused again once they return to their desks.

The third type of cost – incompetent decision-making – is potentially the most serious. I wonder to this day about the potential legal, never mind moral, ramifications of the committee where I inadvertently acquired undue influence. At its worst, and depending on the type of business you are in, the pitfalls of group decision-making can have serious knock-on effects on customer relations, financial results, even life and limb.

## Groups Can Make More Dangerous Mistakes Than Their Individual Members

*Victims of Groupthink* is the name of a hugely sobering book by Irving Janis which looked at the potentially disastrous consequences of the ways groups fall into decision-making ruts. His classic case study looked at the 1961 Bay of Pigs fiasco, in which the USA under President John F. Kennedy got embroiled in a plot to invade Cuba and overthrow Fidel Castro, thus sowing the seeds for the Cuban Missile Crisis, perhaps the nearest the world ever came to nuclear war. The factors which led to the decision come up time and again in more mundane group decision processes, and include:

- Strong "us and them" syndrome

- Undue influence of a minority of members (enforced through subtle or not-so-subtle intimidation)

- Pressure on individuals to conform ("You're either for us or against us")

- Fear to express divergent views, and especially to disagree with someone in authority, even when they are known to be mistaken

By the way, the committee responsible for this was full of highly competent, spectacularly successful individuals including Robert McNamara (among many other achievements, the first person from outside the Ford family to become President of the motor company), and Bobby Kennedy, then Attorney-General, later a senator (who in the following year showed his incredible negotiation abilities in helping resolve the missile crisis – see the film *Thirteen Days*), not to mention several decorated multiple-star generals.

A further dynamic bedevils board meetings and other committees in the business of reviewing proposals: so-called "diffusion of responsibility". It is incredibly easy for a busy board member to feel that the CEO, their expert staff, advisors, and fellow directors have all given a particular proposal adequate scrutiny, with the result that racy ideas get the go-ahead with inadequate consideration of risk. If you have ever been at such a meeting I am sure you know what I am talking about. And if you recall the grilling that members of the RBS board got by MPs, you will be well aware that this can happen at the highest levels of the biggest organizations, just as it can to a local charity board.

Groupthink and diffusion of responsibility are often found at work in accident investigations and inquiries into corporate scandals – for example the Columbia and Challenger shuttle disasters, numerous commercial airliner crashes, the Enron scandal and BP's (lack of) safety culture etc. At best, groupthink makes fools out of individually competent meeting attendees; at worst it wipes out shareholder value and even kills people.

# *Ten Steps To More Productive Meetings*

Perhaps few of us meet regularly to discuss whether to launch an invasion or a space shuttle. But we do decide to launch products, set objectives, allot budgets, appoint people to jobs and plan projects, and the risks in terms of time, money, morale and errors are real. The remedies are straightforward (although it has to be said they require a certain type of discipline which is not always easily mustered).

## 1. Be clear about the difference between political meetings and results-oriented meetings

Politics is an important fact of organizational life, and it is often played out in meetings. It doesn't make sense to complain about this or try to eliminate it, but it is good to be clear about peoples' objectives individually and collectively when agreeing to meet. If the substance of the meeting agenda is secondary to political considerations (jockeying for power and influence, building alliances etc.) then by all means play the game and judge the value of the meeting in political terms. If, however, the substance is important, then don't let politics intervene to the detriment of the organization's objectives.

## 2. Identify desired results before developing an agenda

Agendas are usually a collection of issues thrown together quickly, and items are often vague, nebulous and open-ended. The emphasis is on tasks ("discussing" issues), rather than results. To develop a results-oriented agenda, simply ask:

> "If we discuss this issue, where would we have to get to at the end of the meeting in order for us to say we had used our time well?"

This discipline is simple, but it is not necessarily easy to do. However, it can be surprisingly powerful, and as I know from any number of "facilitation gigs", it is a trusty tool for breaking impasses and getting an organization's leadership moving again.

### 3. Consider alternatives to meeting

Once you are clear on the desired results, the first thing to consider is: "Do we need a meeting at all?" Can the issue be handled by email, on the phone, in a videoconference, by delegation, or even by ignoring it? It is easy to quantify the potential savings. A well-focused single issue conference call can sort out in twenty minutes (with no travel time either side) an issue that can lead you round the houses all afternoon in person.

### 4. Agree what evidence will let you know an item has been handled properly – beware the seduction of timed agendas

Timed agendas are promoted as a way of saving time. But they make no sense unless the only purpose of the meeting is to be able to claim that an issue has been discussed (i.e. the meeting is political and may as well be done as quickly as possible). While a rough estimate may be possible, how can anyone know in advance how long an issue requiring genuine discussion will take to reach satisfactory closure?

### 5. Don't try to handle too many issues at one meeting

If the discussion of an item doesn't reach closure, the tendency is that it becomes "Chair's action" (in which case why did it need a meeting in the first place), or it gets held over to the next meeting and the whole discussion gets opened up again. Prioritise items (various well-thought out methods for doing this exist), and pick a very few. Have a reserve list in case there is time left over – I bet you'll never need it.

## 6. Establish and uphold ground-rules to avoid time-wasting diversions

For example, once everyone has agreed on the outcome the meeting is to achieve, a context has been set in which anything which does not contribute is irrelevant. You can now set up a time-saving rule: if someone can't justify the relevance of a point when challenged, they must drop it (and pursue it at another time if they wish).

## 7. Use decision-making processes which headoff groupthink

Many workable processes exist or can be devised. What's important is to collect contributions from all participants, apply consistent and reasonable criteria for weighing objectives, challenge assumptions and ensure that dominant personalities do not bias the conversation.

## 8. Be systematic in your appraisal of risks, and make preventative and contingent actions standard features of plans

In meetings I observe, risk is often handled haphazardly. Certainly, experienced managers and directors will raise questions of risk, but it is done informally, with the result than vulnerable areas can slip through the net (there is also sometimes the pressure not to raise too many such questions in one meeting to avoid being perceived as "negative"). The advice recommended years ago by Kepner and Tregoe in their book *The Rational Manager* is timeless. Make it a standard practice to have a formal scan that looks for vulnerable areas in the plan, identifies specific issues, and then sets up preventive and contingent ("insurance") actions in advance.

## 9. Ensure follow-through

Many people have observed that "strategies never fail at the formulation stage" and the same is true of any decisions, plans or resolutions made at meetings. Lack of follow-through promotes cynicism. How will the group ensure that its decisions are implemented? Make this explicit in defining actions.

## 10. Consider bringing in skilled facilitation

The recommendations above could amount to a lot of work for a busy executive. And it's difficult to participate fully in discussions and attend to the process at the same time. For important meetings, away days and retreats, or when a team is going to be working together over a long period, there's a lot to be said for getting specialist outside support.

A good facilitator is someone who:

- allows to you and your people to focus on the substantive content rather than also try to manage the process

- keeps the meeting on track towards its objective

- can bring the necessary discipline, because they have a single focus (they don't have any agenda other than a successful meeting)

- is not affected by internal politics, or intimidated by the relative seniority of some attendees over others

- will solicit contributions from reticent people and ensure dominant ones don't steal the show or bias the proceedings

- acts as an honest broker, and can get agreement on relevance and priority issues

- acts as a referee and upholds ground-rules

- can take you through decision-making processes that head off groupthink

- ensures that risks receive thorough consideration without being perceived as negative
- provides an external check that actions have sufficient accountability

## *Final Thoughts*

Poor meetings waste time and money, negatively affect morale and can lead to bad decisions with worse consequences. Groups can easily fall prey to patterns which lead even the most competent individuals to be party to wasteful, silly, and even dangerous actions.

The processes of good meetings are well understood and can produce dramatic improvements in organizational effectiveness. Because it can be hard to attend to both the substantive issues and the demands of a good process, it is often worth bringing in a skilled facilitator from elsewhere in the organization, or from the outside.

# CHAPTER FIFTEEN

# How To Accelerate Implementation by Influencing Across Departments

One of the most frustrating and wasteful drags on implementation speed arises when teams having to wait for people in other internal departments to do things. When this occurs, people may conclude that the other party doesn't care, isn't interested, lacks appropriate urgency or is even trying to undermine the project for political reasons.

Sometimes that is the case, but usually the reasons are much more innocent, and in fact not only are the "guilty parties" perfectly competent and conscientious, they have been wondering why *the other party* is so difficult and unresponsive!

The result is an "us and them" situation where both sides waste time complaining in their own camps, and trying to pass the buck up the line to their respective managers to sort out. Those same managers, if they are wise, will refuse to be drawn into refereeing and will instead insist that frontline leaders step up and start expediting matters for themselves.

## *People's Perception is Their Reality*

The trick to getting other groups to do things is the same as the trick for all successful influence: you have to see and understand the world from the other party's perspective.

When you try to explain other people's lack of responsiveness from your own point of view, it is hard for three reasons:

- **"Out of sight, out of mind"**: We find it hard to appreciate the demands on people not in our sight. And we tend to assume that nothing else they have to do is as important as our project.

- **What is obvious to you is not necessarily obvious to them:** We tend to assume they know what we know, believe what we believe, and will therefore quite naturally act as we think they should. Therefore if they haven't done their part, we start to suspect it must be deliberate.

- **The mind has a built in bias:** Psychologists tell us that we see our own slippages as the results of external factors beyond our control, whereas we tend to see those of others as being the results of their lack of competence. Enlightened Zen Masters excepted, we all do this at times and it takes practice and vigilance to set the bias aside.

These tendencies mean that we can find it easier to assume deliberate obstruction – and team members will tend to reinforce that view around the water cooler. *Result*: a self-sealing "us and them" perspective which just slows things down further.

Again, think about it from the other side: has anybody ever assumed that *you* were being obstructive when you were just hugely busy?

A caveat: sometimes, of course, obstruction *is* deliberate. Then you might want to get out the big guns. But it's far better not to jump to that conclusion before testing for something more innocent.

# Ten Ways To Improve
# Influence Across Departments

Here's a range of tactics for expediting projects, negotiating silos and generally managing "stakeholders". Some focus on tasks and some on relationships. You don't need to do them all. In fact it's best to pick the one or two which most suit the situation and the people you are dealing with. Make sure your project teams are familiar with these principles:

## 1. Sell it from *their* point of view

How will helping you help them? Will it make their scheduling easier, make them look good, or even just get you off their back?

## 2. Identify the natural conditions under which they would willingly help you, and act to establish them

Ask yourself: "Under what circumstances would the other person do what I want naturally and quickly?" For example, if your accounts payable policy is to accept any early payment discounts offered, and your order is being sat on by the relevant functionary, say "I need your help to take this discount for early payment before it expires."

## 3. Identify in advance what and who could stall your project, and put plan-protecting actions (both "preventive" and "contingent/insurance") into place

For example, if you know from past experience that a particular manager has a talent for raising annoying queries which hold projects up (perhaps as a way of feeling important) you are going to need to use some guile. Speak to them way before they are scheduled to be involved in the project to get their input – ask *them* to tell you all the potential problems with your plans and ask for recommendations (preventive action). Then ask them if you may call on them to help troubleshoot any unforeseen issues that inevitably will arise in a project of this nature (insurance action).

### 4. Clarify responsibilities and nail down potential ambiguities

When you said you needed it by Friday, what precisely are you asking them to agree to? Are you thinking lunchtime, while they are thinking 5.15 pm?

### 5. Create obligations by confirming the resources you are mobilising

For example: send an email saying, "Thanks for agreeing to X. I'm visiting the client on Friday and will incorporate your comments while I am on the train so please can you confirm you will get them to me by noon."

### 6. Make it easy for them to do what you want

One of the secrets of success in direct marketing, and websites such as Amazon, is to make it really easy for people to respond. You can use the same ideas to expedite your project – it's a little more work for you, but if they are very busy or very senior, it can make the difference, so it could still be worth it. Simple example: if you are chasing someone who is supposed to phone you to discuss a document, include the document again when you chase them, and send your phone number again too. Just forward the original email and include your signature file. If you don't do this, the other person has to look back though their inbox to find the document, dig your phone number out etc. They are more likely to put it on a to-do list where it will languish for days.

## 7. Influence the influencers

Even if you are very senior, in a large matrix organization, you may not be able to influence the blocking party directly. But someone can. Figure out early on who has the requisite clout: it may be their boss, it may be a mutual friend, it may be an informal opinion leader in their department who has influence just by virtue of personality, and it will often be a secretary. Build an informal influence network and use it.

## 8. Work with gatekeepers and assistants

I am sometimes amazed by the lack of astuteness of people who are rude to, or dismissive of, gatekeepers and assistants. It is unacceptable behaviour in itself, but it is also plain daft. Secretaries can get all sorts of things fast-tracked, or alternatively cause them to languish at the bottom of an in-tray.

## 9. Invest in relationships "offline"

It's easy, as we have noted, to fall into the trap of assuming that the other person is blocking you on purpose. Often they are just snowed under themselves. Taking the time to build a relationship with them helps in two ways: a) you realise that they are unlikely to be blocking you on purpose; b) you have more influence when you need it.

## 10. Involve them in your plan protection – once you have a good relationship

This is the ideal situation. Early in the project you get together and discuss the sorts of issues mentioned above *together*. Remember to couch it in their best interest: "Look I know your team members are really busy and I'd like to see if we can find ways to smooth out the inevitable demands this project will create. Shall we get together and figure out how to make it go as easily as possible?" Then work out your plan promoting and plan protecting actions together. Arrange a "red telephone" so you can call if there's a problem.

## *But This Seems Like a Lot of Work!*

Does this seem like a lot of work? It does to me. One manager said to me in frustration: "Why can't they *just do it?*" Here are three things to bear in mind:

1.  Good management always involves thinking through potential problems and creating the best conditions for success – this is no different.

2.  What's your alternative? Stakeholder risks to your project need to be managed just like any other risk, and if you don't bother, you are conceding unnecessary control of your success to others.

3.  As you build your relationships across organizational boundaries, things get much easier and more streamlined – the upfront investment pays off down the line.

## *Final Thoughts*

In the Introduction, I said that leaders have to be vigilant about warranting "them and us" conversations. In doing so, you are working to control a pretty basic tendency: people like to belong to tribes. Great leaders have always unified internal warring factions of course, and when they have succeeded, it's by getting people focused outside the organization ('them' becomes the competition, or even better, 'them' becomes the people or forces making your customers' lives more difficult).

## LESSONS ABOUT TURF WARS FROM *CSI MIAMI*

The trouble with turf wars is that everyone's energy is focused internally – on the organization and its politics – rather than externally on the customer or client. This can only be bad for business.

Detective fiction can offer valuable management lessons – especially in regard to the power of evidence over assumptions. In the section on Leadership, I advocate the Columbo Technique for dealing with under-performance. I was delighted to find another lesson – one that points to a way to defeat value-destroying problems such as turf wars, in-fighting in management teams and the "not-invented here" syndrome.

This time the source was *CSI Miami* (Series 2, episode 47).

In this episode, Horatio (David Caruso) has to follow a lead from Miami to Manhattan, and quickly bumps into his New York counterpart Mac (Gary Sinise). The scene in which the two investigative aces meet for the first time is striking.

Here are the key occurrences:

**Horatio appears on Mac's territory at a crime scene connected to their two independent investigations. They have never met before. They are both senior, and are local heroes on their own patch. Clearly, they have a potential jurisdictional clash. However, they avoid the clash totally and work together to resolve both cases.**

They focus on the question of how to maximise the value they are pursuing (in this case, justice), rather than starting by defending their status in an organizational structure (geographically-defined turf).

**Horatio notes that Mac is using a different procedure from his own for the vital task of collecting evidence to take the lab. He remarks on it, but without any kind of judgemental connotation. Mac explains that the New York method is an alternative way of achieving the same principled aims as the Miami method. Horatio says 'interesting', and they move on.**

They are interested in producing the best result possible, and are open to alternative methods and improved practices.

> **Mac's assistant enters. Mac makes it clear that they are on the same side. The assistant immediately accepts this and gives full assistance to both Mac and Horatio.**
>
> Mac has the trust of his assistant. His say-so is enough to vouch for Horatio. And he has inculcated a reason-based, results-oriented sense of priorities in his staff rather than a them-and-us bunker mentality.
>
> All three characters have strong egos. In fact their egos are so strong that they don't need to shout about it. Because of their rationality, clarity of values, and strong self-esteem, they navigate the situation in a way that is strikingly different from most TV drama plots, and I'd suggest from many analogous real-life encounters.
>
> Of course, it's an idealised situation – one of the great values of fiction is its potential to project a view of life as it could be – but actually it's nothing more (or less) than professionalism should really demand.
>
> **Questions to think about**
>
> - Does your culture promote evidence and reason over assumptions and unarticulated feelings?
> - Do your incentive systems make the kind of cooperation portrayed impossible?
> - Are people clear enough on their responsibilities to stakeholders, and particularly customers/clients, to confidently negotiate potential "jurisdictional clashes"?

---

> ### WHY DON'T THEY DO WHAT I ASK?
>
> Have you ever said to yourself: I have told them a million times, why don't they:
>
> - Come up with innovating ideas?
> - Act more entrepreneurially?
> - Sell the new product line rather than the old one?
> - Look after existing profitable clients, and not just chase after new ones?
> - Go networking more often?

- Challenge me when I am wrong, or at least offer me another perspective?

If you want to understand why people don't do what you need them to, even when they have explicitly agreed that they will, the answer will usually be found by working out the informal incentives. These incentives may be financial, but they are at least as often other factors such as peer acceptance, job security and freedom from micromanagement.

Here's a topical example: risk management in banks – with thanks to a couple of risk managers from a well-known London-based bank which must remain nameless. (Although the example is from investment banking, you'll find the same process behind other problems, from the dramatic, such as transport accidents and governance scandals, to the common or garden such as excessive employee turnover or "creative" sales reporting.)

The crucial thing to understand about risk managers is this: they are rewarded when they say everything is okay and there is nothing too much to worry about, and *they are punished when they identify risks*. Here's how this works:

Let's say you are a risk manager and you have identified a risky position that your bank has taken. Do you speak up or not? If you don't speak up when you perceive an issue, and the nasty risk doesn't happen, you'll have toed the line and been a good team-player, i.e. you'll get a (powerful, informal) *reward*. If the problem actually occurs, you have no more chance of losing your job than anybody else, because your extensive records show that you produced vast amounts of daily analysis and got a green audit report: *reward*, or at least neutral.

In fact, if it all goes wrong and you haven't warned of the risks, you have a better chance of keeping your job than most people because the bank will need risk managers to shut the stable door after the horse has bolted, as a demonstration to auditors, regulators and investors that the bank has a zealous risk management function: *reward*.

If, however, you speak up and the bad scenario doesn't transpire, you'll be accused of crying wolf and not having a business perspective: *punishment*. Do this a few times and it will be extremely "career limiting", as people at HBOS discovered, for example: *punishment*.

What about the fourth possibility: you correctly warn of a risk? Well, then you probably still get punished, because there's usually a delay between a warning and the event. During the delay, you still get treated like you are crying wolf, and then if it happens and they didn't listen to you, you are an embarrassment.

My source said this: "Remember that a risk manager is supposed to talk about risk – the nasties that probably won't happen, but might. There's supposed to be an organizational culture that supports you, saying, 'Look, there's too much risk here, we've got to reduce or hedge our exposure', but in reality you reduce your personal income and job security by doing anything other than rubber stamping everything. And most of the time, everything will turn out alright – even when it doesn't, the risk manager is unlikely to take the blame."

**What does this mean for your business?**

Why don't risk managers speak up? Well, would you?

What about your organization? If you're a leader racking your brains trying to understand why people say and agree to one thing, and then do another, I'm willing to bet the answer is in the *informal* incentives. Find out what *really* happens when people do or don't do what the business needs from them. Are those consequences encouraging the behaviour you need, or undermining it? What needs to change?

If you're "the boss", it can be very hard to get the answers to these questions (again the reason is that the incentives, or at least the perceived incentives, work against people telling you) so you might need to engage some outside help.

# CHAPTER SIXTEEN

# LEADERSHIP:
# LESS ABOUT CHARISMA,
# MORE ABOUT BEHAVIOUR

Organizations have a keen need for leadership at all levels. And judging by the turn out at presentations I give on the subject, many people are interested in *being* leaders. However, much of what is written and said on the subject focuses unhelpfully on "charismatic leadership". While charisma is undoubtedly a powerful force, it's hard to see the value of a lot of this punditry for budding leaders, or the organizations that need them, for the following reasons:

- Charisma is in the eye of the beholder. Here are some names often considered charismatic: Nelson Mandela, Bill Clinton, Tony Blair, Barack Obama, Elvis Presley, The Dalai Lama. First, you may agree or disagree with these names, for example, many people can see it in Mandela, but find that Blair leaves them cold.

- Just because people will follow you doesn't mean you are going in a good direction – some people experienced Osama Bin Laden as charismatic, as others did Benito Mussolini.

- Even if charisma is a leadership asset, it's doubtful it can be cultivated. I am sure you can help people become more socially skilled and better at interpersonal influence, but truly charismatic? The results of such attempts will more likely resemble Woody Allen getting ready for a date by making James Bond faces in the mirror.

- We need leadership *at all levels* in our organizations: can you imagine the chaos in a firm managed exclusively by clones of Nelson Mandela, Richard Branson or Alan Sugar? A good premise for a comedy sketch perhaps, but not likely to lead to effective performance.

It's much more effective to focus, not on ephemeral, hard-to-pin-down qualities with a dubious link to the desired result, but on observable, learnable behaviours, to ask:

- "What do effective leaders *do*?", and
- "How can you get more of your people in your organization doing the same?"

## Leadership is About Results

Here's a very pragmatic definition of leadership behaviour from James Cash Penney, founder of the US retail chain which bears his name: "My definition of an executive's job is brief and to the point. It is simply this: getting things done through other people." This might not be the whole story on leadership, but it has some important virtues:

- Everyone can understand it and agree on what it means
- You can measure it
- You can improve it in a clear and incontrovertible way

The ability to get things done through other people is vital, and its absence is a major limit to the growth of businesses and of individual careers. If you can't confidently delegate responsibility for results, you can't think and act strategically, and if you can't act strategically, your direction will be determined by the competition, the economy, your customers, your suppliers, your employees, and who knows what other random factors – hardly a position of leadership.

# Why is Getting Things Done Through Other People Difficult?

Anyone who has tried it knows that getting things done through other people can be extraordinarily difficult, even when the request is reasonable, the other person has the capability, and they say to your face that they are willing to do it. You usually can't just order them. The only organizations where that approach works tend to be military ones. If you are in the Parachute Regiment, for example, an order to jump out of a C130 is formally an order from the Queen, so you'd better jump. It is what you signed up to.

Such conditions don't any longer obtain outside the military, if they ever did. Businesses are less formal and less hierarchical. People are much less deferential than they were only a few decades ago. Rightly or wrongly, the reason "because the boss says so" doesn't cut much ice these days.

So if you can't order them, how about employing carrots and sticks? (or Reward Power and Coercive Power in the terms of French and Raven's famous Five Bases of Power). This sounds more promising: decide what you want people to do and then "motivate" them through rewards and punishments. Carrots and sticks will definitely get people to do things. The problem is, as Alan Weiss's visual in Figure 16.1 illustrates, you have to keep providing the rewards and punishments in order to maintain the desired direction and interdict the undesired one. The task-master is kept as busy as the slaves.

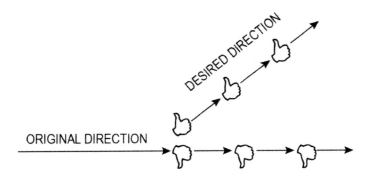

Figure 16.1: Compliance demands constant reinforcement
(adapted from Alan Weiss)

As Alan points out, you don't motivate people this way, you just move them. There is no basis for that vitally needed delegation here – the task-master has to constantly "micromanage". And no delegation means severe limits on your ability to grow your business.

Here's the nub of the issue in a nutshell: you *can't* motivate people (I love causing audiences' eyes to pop out with this observation).

In truth, people are already motivated – even the ones you think are not. The laziest good-for-nothing is motivated: to avoid hassle, responsibility and effort. You can *move* them with threats or bribes, but that's as good as it will get until they decide their priorities have changed.

On the other hand, your best employee is also motivated: perhaps to pursue a rewarding career, contribute to an exciting, worthwhile enterprise, support family members etc. These motivations are already there, and a good leader taps into them.

## *The Leader as an Educator*

The origin of the word *educate* is in the idea: "to draw out". And it's extremely useful to think about leadership as a process of education – tapping into the latent motivation and talent within your people. Lest this seems touchy-feely, consider that education systems were a major, explicit plank of Jack Welch's huge success at GE. Listen to him interviewed, and it is clear that Welch is a vocational educator. And no-one ever accused "Neutron Jack" of being touchy-feely.

Clients find the following framework very helpful as they learn to "get things done through other people", and as they commensurately teach their followers to accept the required accountability. It is only one way of looking at leadership behaviour of course (although as I like to joke in presentations, it does enjoy the particular virtue of being the correct one).

The framework comes from Paul Hersey and Ken (*One Minute Manger*) Blanchard and is called Situational Leadership. The idea is that you vary your objectives and behaviour with your people according to what stage in their development (the "situation") they have reached – see Figure 16.2.

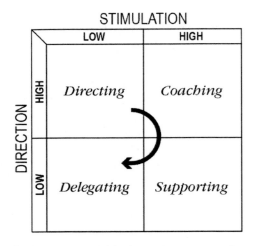

Figure 16.2: Adapting your leadership to the situation. Adapted from
Hersey & Blanchard, *Management of Organizational Behaviour*

The framework looks at the *range* of possible leader behaviours in terms of a) how directing they are, and b) how much stimulation they provide to subordinates. The four combinations are sequenced in a path that takes the follower from being a complete novice to being someone to whom assignments can be safely delegated, i.e. someone trusted to accept and discharge responsibility for producing results – in short, an executive. The four stages are as follows:

1. **Directing:** At this first stage, the new subordinate is given a specific, clearly defined task to complete, and is then left to get on with it on their own. If you learn tennis, as an analogy, the instructor may show you how to hold a racket and bounce a ball, and then leave you to practise until you have some semblance of coordination. In a business setting, a junior may be given straightforward tasks to do – researching, checking information, getting quotes from a range of suppliers, coordinating meetings etc.

2.  **Coaching:** Now the person has acquired some skills, they are given interactive support in integrating and applying it to increasingly challenging concrete situations. To continue the tennis analogy, an instructor may hit balls across the net, deliberately working your forehand or backhand, helping you to integrate individual skills into a whole package. In our business example, perhaps the junior drafts a report for a client, and is then coached intensively by their supervisor on structure, style, strength of the business case etc.

3.  **Supporting:** At this stage, the leader takes a keen interest in performance, and offers encouragement, but is much slower to intervene with instructions. Your tennis instructor might play a game against you, or watch and encourage while you play another student. At this point, an increasingly confident professional might be left to produce a final draft which will then receive approval, or fairly cursory corrective feedback. The supervisor may make themselves available for input if required, but doesn't constantly monitor every detail.

4.  **Delegating:** The leader gives responsibility for producing results to the subordinate, who accepts that responsibility within some agreed boundaries – budgetary, contractual, policy, regulatory etc. See the box below for a practical framework. To continue the tennis analogy, the player in a competition is on their own. Their coach and sponsors observes from the sidelines but do not, indeed cannot, influence the play in real time. In a business situation, the leader may delegate responsibility for delivering a client project, or managing a product line, an office or client relationship, thus freeing them to develop the business strategically.

When I have coached people on their delegation skills, the first issue that usually comes up is not the person's unwillingness to let go of control *per se*, but their fear that if they do let go of control their people are not prepared to take accountability for results. Thinking in terms of situational leadership provides an explicit map to develop the required qualities in your people over time.

In my work with leaders, I will often ask them to identify which quadrants their relationships with subordinates fall into, and we will then plan how they can accelerate the progress of their people through the process.

The transitions most emerging leaders find hard are the ones from Coaching to Supporting and especially to Delegating. Here are seven suggestions that have proven useful:

## Seven Keys for Developing Subordinates to Take Accountability

### 1. Set *developmental* objectives and choose/change your style as required

Before any suitable interaction, don't just think about the immediate business task you want performed. Take a moment to identify the developmental stage of the person you are working with. Do you tend to direct them, making a rod for your own back, when actually they are more than ready to take on the whole job? Do they need so much coaching, or could they be left to their own devices more? Which of the following ideas might help to move them on to the next stage?

## 2. Consider the trade-offs between *telling* and *asking*

Sir John Whitmore makes a great observation about the power of Asking over Telling in performance coaching. A standard instruction to players of all ball sports is to "keep your eye on the ball". Sometimes it works, but often only temporarily – you have to keep reminding them. You will get much better results if, as a tennis coach for example, you ask questions such as, "Which way is the ball spinning as it comes over the net?" In order to answer the question, the coachee has to get much more *involved* in the performance, they discover more for themselves, and it tends therefore to stick.

## 3. Question their premises rather than showing them their errors

If you are experienced, you may already know how the task should be done. But if you simply tell someone all the angles, you rob them of vital learning experiences, and their knowledge remains superficial, limiting their ability to act in new situations. Rather than saying in response to their suggestion, "That doesn't work because of X, Y and Z", compare the effects of this simple switch: ask "What are the likely side-effects of that course of action?" or "How can you minimise any down-side?"

## 4. Consider the trade-offs between *suggesting alternatives* and *offering perspectives*

The idea is to let them discover the answer for themselves. Sometimes it is much more powerful to say, "Your situation reminds me of a time when... Does that help you in thinking about this issue?" and let them do the work.

## 5. Encourage long-range thinking

Leaders have to think long-range. Often subordinates are thinking over the very short run – their preoccupation is the immediate problem. Create a wider context, and a consideration of fundamental priorities and values, by asking about long term effects and consequences of decisions. For example, when coaching people who have "rotated into" departmental management roles, I have always been concerned to ensure some consideration of life once they rotate *out* again. I don't want their ultimate career trajectory hurt because they were too distracted with short-term demands of internal politics and routine administration for three years.

## 6. Keep an eye on life-balance

There are many ways to apportion the life balance pie, and individuals vary tremendously: one person's balance might feel like a 45 degree list to starboard for someone else. I am not suggesting that a leader should be intrusive but, especially when you have a mentoring-type relationship, it's appropriate to make suggestions to protect people from burnout – especially ambitious, driven, conscientious individuals.

## 7. Create or suggest challenges

Remember that sometimes, the most powerful thing a leader or mentor can say to someone is, "Yes, you should have a go at that."

# Final Thoughts

There's no doubting the power of charisma, and leaders who have it certainly have an asset (if they can figure out what to do with it).

But there is a more fundamental aspect of leadership. With or without charisma, leaders at all levels in organizations need to constantly learn and improve their ability to get results through their people.

Furthermore, they then need to help their reports do the same thing. This is not a process of bossing people about, either through direct orders or using carrots and sticks. It is fundamentally an educational process – a process of drawing out the potential of people by helping them learn to deliver results.

Leaders create leaders.

---

### HOW TO DELEGATE

If you want to get results through other people, then you need to delegate. In doing so, it's extremely helpful to have a framework. Here is my REWARDS™ format for delegation. REWARDS stands for:

1. **R**esults
2. **E**vidence
3. **W**hy?
4. Make an **A**greement
5. Negotiate **R**esources
6. **D**ocument the agreement
7. **S**upport

And finally,

8. REWARD success.

I've used them very successfully with coaching clients – here are the steps in more detail.

---

**1. Specify the *results* you want, not the method, and hold people responsible for the result.**

In the words of General George Patton, "Don't tell people how to do things, tell them what to do and let them surprise you with their results". As well as benefiting from their ingenuity, there's another plus: if you are too specific about the route to achieving a goal and there turn out to be unforeseen roadblocks, some people will give up and dump it back at your door: "You told me to go this way, and it didn't work, so I give up – over to you." If you have specified the *destination*, not the route, then the onus remains on them to find their way – it's reasonable for them to request extra help, but not to give up.

**2. Specify *evidence* – how will you both know for sure that you got the result?**

Here's a common, and very annoying problem: you ask someone to do something, and what you get is not what you wanted, but you can see how they got the wrong end of the stick. You end up settling for what you didn't want, or having the work done over – an annoying waste of time. Usually the culprit is vague language. Make it absolutely clear what you want to *see*, *hear* and/or *feel* that will confirm the result. For example, "What I am really after is a one page press release on my desk, with all the right facts and contact details already filled in, that makes the reader feel like they want to get on the phone for the story immediately."

**3. Make it clear *why* the result is important at *two levels* of objective above.**

Individual jobs, especially staff jobs which are similar even in different industries – HR, Accounts, IT, Estates – can seem quite disconnected from the strategy of the business. Make it plain how the result you are requesting contributes to ultimate performance. It helps people get motivated, it shows how your request is reasonable, and it enables them to improvise if they come up against problems.

**4. Make it plain that you are proposing a contract, or *agreement* – ask them if they accept.**

You can coerce people to do things, but that's not delegation. This step is the crucial moment where responsibility is delegated. You ask them (explicitly or implicitly), "Are you prepared to sign up to this? If you do, you are accountable." Be vigilant that they don't accept too automatically. Consider playing devil's advocate. If they are more junior, this is a big opportunity to coach and develop them.

**5. Allow the assignee to negotiate changes to the specification, including *resources and support*.**

Ideally you want someone who says, "Yes, I can make this happen for you, as long as I have the following resources."

**6. *Document* the agreement.**

A simple email will be enough in some cases; in others, something more akin to a project proposal, with milestones, metrics etc. is needed.

**7. Monitor and *support*, but don't solve all their problems for them.**

There's a difference between delegation and abdication.

**8. On completion, acknowledge result and give out *rewards*, if appropriate.**

This doesn't have to be a big deal, but it shouldn't be skipped either. Since real motivation is intrinsic, the best reward comes from helping the person feel personal satisfaction and an increasing sense of competence.

## CHAPTER SEVENTEEN

# GIVING FEEDBACK, TAKING FEEDBACK

"Let me give you some feedback." If we are honest, these are not words most of us like hearing, especially when they are offered unsolicited. We know it's somehow important, but that doesn't mean we like it.

Actually the term 'feedback' is much misunderstood and has been diluted and distorted from its original meaning. We need to recover that meaning, because real feedback is vital steering and learning information, and without it both individual performance and overall leadership effectiveness can be severely compromised, as many failures attest (think BP, HBOS, or the major banks that dealt with Bernie Madoff).

As a leader or an ambitious individual contributor, it's vital to make sure you create effective feedback loops for yourself first, and then for the rest of the organization. That might mean confronting some discomfort, but not half as much as if you cut yourself off from the stuff.

Oh, and if we want feedback about our business operations, we have to resist the temptation to shoot the messenger!

## *How Poorly-Given Feedback Undermines Individual and Organizational Performance*

Most so-called feedback is actually no such thing, and generally does little to help performance (it may actually undermine it). Here are the three most common types of 'imposter-feedback':

## Opinion masquerades as feedback which creates unreality and dependence

Here's a typical exchange:

> Manager: "That was a great presentation."

> Staff member: "Thank you."

The manager walks away congratulating themselves on offering praise and "catching people doing things right" etc. But, did the staff member really receive much of value? A bit of recognition, fair enough. Reinforcement, you might say? Hmm, to reinforce what? How do they know what to repeat next time? Since they don't know, how can they take responsibility for their own performance when you are not there to tell them?

## Ill-thought-out attempts are made to measure performance

As a child growing up during the later years of the Cold War, I remember wondering what use the 'four minute warning' of impending nuclear attack actually served (and occasionally, being terrified by factor sirens)? What could we actually do on receipt of the warning? Organizations are full of signals that suggest people should be responding to something, but without a clue as to what the response should be. Think of all those forms (for example in the appraisal process, at the end of workshops or on customer 'feedback' forms) that ask you to do the following sorts of things:

**How would you rate Mary's work attitude?**
*1   2   3   4   5   6   7   8   9   10*

**How would you rate the content of the session?**
*1   2   3   4   5   6   7   8   9   10*

**How did we do?**
*1   2   3   4   5   6   7   8   9   10*

We all fill these in – but is it helping the person receiving it? What is anyone supposed to do with the number? How can the recipient adjust their actions? Are they just supposed to vary their behaviour randomly next time and see if it works better? And if it does, how can they tell which bit of behaviour to keep this time? This is worse than useless, not only because it is pure non-productive busy work, but more insidiously because it is a clear message that "going through the motions is okay round here." The most likely response is disengagement and drift, and more going through the motions.

### 'Feedback' sessions become an excuse to verbally beat people up, damaging morale

Humanistic ideology has pervaded organizational life, and often opens the door for passive aggression. If you 'should be open to feedback', then someone can beat you up verbally, and then blame you for being defensive when you react badly. People who perceive a threat to their ego respond with hostility or stress, thereby learning nothing and starting to wonder about revising their CV.

## *What Feedback Really is, and What it is Not*

*Feedback is steering information, not opinions, evaluations or judgements.* Actually that's the whole thing in a nutshell, and in a way, the rest of this chapter is simply a commentary and illustration of this key idea. Here's why it matters:

- Steering information is not threatening. It is descriptive – not evaluative, judgemental or capricious.

- Steering information is not a matter of biased opinion – it can be validated objectively.

- Steering information is incredibly valuable for all kinds of performance improvement at the individual as well as organizational level.

---

**THE SCIENTIFIC BASIS: IT'S ALL GREEK TO ME**

I'm not just wildly asserting that people have got the wrong idea about the idea of *feedback*. It's a technical concept with a precise and quite simple meaning. Correctly understood it's a powerful way to manage and improve performance. The term comes from a multi-disciplinary field with a very descriptive name: descriptive that is if you speak ancient Greek! The field is called *cybernetics* – the name of which literally translates as "the art of the steersman". Think of the sailor with the oar over the back of a Spartan ship sailing to Troy, maintaining course by keeping the mast aligned with a star. The ship is constantly being diverted by the wind and the waves – *feedback*[7] is the process which makes successful navigation possible. So what is it?

One of the pioneers of cybernetics, Heinz von Foerster, defined feedback as: *The return of part of a system's output to change its input.* In other words: when the star drifts to the left relative to the mast, that is feedback that the oar is too much to the right. The sailor can recognise his behaviour (the way he is holding the oar) and its effect in the world (the drifting of the star to the left) and adjust accordingly.

The Captain could stand by the navigator all night saying "That's good", or "That's bad", or "I rate you as a 6/10 steersman", but it wouldn't help performance one iota. *The performer must recognise their own behaviour and its effect in the world.*

---

[7] A word to the wise: I am actually only talking about one kind of feedback here: corrective (a.k.a. balancing, negative) feedback.

## *Poor Attempts at Feedback*

Because of the half-understood influence of some great management thinkers, everyone agrees feedback is important even though they don't agree what it is (no-one ever says: "Feedback is over-rated – let's not bother with it."). So things happen which get called feedback but are at best poor imitations:

- **Attempting to give feedback when the receiver isn't involved in an active learning process with you.** The words "I have some feedback for you" are words likely to induce heart-sink in most people. In order for feedback – as opposed to 'correction' or 'punishment' – to be effective, people have got to be actively engaged in a goal-seeking or learning process (motivation is intrinsic: the steersman has to be interested in getting to the destination, and really should be getting a kick out of improving their ability to hold an accurate course – the worse the weather, the better). If your message to someone about their performance is unsolicited or unwelcome, it's likely to be filtered out at best, or resented at worst. If the receiver isn't actively trying to steer somewhere, they will not thank you for your contribution.

  **The clumsy feedback sandwich.** This well-known "communication technique" is an attempt to make a message more palatable, on the Mary Poppins principle that a spoonful of sugar makes the medicine go down. You say something nice, then you give the feedback (which is presupposed by the entire idea to be a criticism), then you say something else nice. It's a technique which has always struck me as manipulative and, because it is also easy to spot, counterproductive to its aim – if the receiver feels manipulated they are hardly likely to be responsive. One of my coaching clients remarked that when he hears someone saying something positive about his performance, he typically starts bracing himself.

- **Vague and imprecise information.** Even assuming the person is open to your contribution, you need to give them something they can use. The vague abstractions of typical management dialogue ("You need to be more proactive") won't cut it. Another pioneer of in this area, Gregory Bateson, called information "difference which makes a difference". Rating a service 6/10 doesn't give the person responsible much to go on. One organization I worked with had the following standard question on their session 'feedback' forms:

  **How well will this session help you in your future career?**
  *1 2 3 4 5 6 7 8 9 10*

  This expects the respondent to be clairvoyant, and the recipient of the feedback to be a mind-reader.

## *Leader, Know Thyself*

Like the archetypal steersman, someone can only treat incoming information as feedback if they are actively engaged in pursuing some goal. Feedback is something you actively get, before it is something you give. So let's start with refining the way we seek and use feedback for ourselves to improve our own performance. If that weren't interesting enough, we will then be in a far better position to ensure great feedback for others, and for the whole organization.

## Five keys to getting effective feedback for yourself

1.  **Set your own goals and performance standards.** Remember that feedback is something you actively seek and get. Therefore you must set, or at least negotiate and thoroughly buy into, your own objectives. There's a reason why almost all coaches, consultants and performance experts emphasise goal setting, whether they think about it this way or not: once you have a properly set objectives, you have created the conditions for feedback-guided success.

2.  **Balance your learning objectives and achievement objectives.** Ultimately you are compensated for achievements, not for learning for the sake of it; however, you won't achieve much if you don't continuously learn new things – so you need both. The steersman wants to successfully navigate to the destination, and to improve their skills along the way.

3.  **Be clear as to how you will ensure you can recognise your actions in the output.** This is the necessary sophistication that makes goal-setting really work. Get good at setting objectives and tracking measures in 'sensory' terms. Demand of yourself that you specify observable behaviour and evidence in the environment. A handy way to approach this is to formulate *video descriptions*. Imagine you are being shadowed by a film crew. What will you see and hear on the playback that will prove you are on-course or off-course?

4.  **Avoid dysfunctional perfectionism by setting min-max goals.** Success is usually a matter of degree more than a matter of absolutes. Ambitious goals are great, but don't be like the parent of my friend who said: "You got three As and a B – are

you going to stay in school another year to turn the B into an A?" He was qualified to go to any university in the land at that point having achieved comfortably within the min-max range required. Job done. Similarly, going into any business meeting or discussion – be it in a complex sale, negotiation or organizational change project for example – the max is usually easy to specify, but do you also take the time to clarify what is the minimum objective that constitutes progress?

5.  **Use the 3Q formula to build on strength and bounce back from disappointment.** Ask yourself the three coaching questions:

    1.  What did I do that worked?
    2.  What did I do better than last time?
    3.  What do I want to work on next?

I learned these from a top football coach.They work amazingly well (the real accelerator questions is number 2, because it creates *amplifying* feedback – literally a "runaway success") both to tell your brain to continue to focus on what is working, and to frame disappointing results in as constructive a light as possible.

## Involving others as a source of feedback

So far all the techniques rely on you getting your own feedback without help – consistent with the ideal of self-mastery. However, we must acknowledge our need for outside input too, or else all we end up with are our own voices echoing around our heads. That way madness lies, as high-profile political and business leaders demonstrate all too often. Involving others is an art: here are three key considerations.

1. **Be careful who you ask.** Consider a) their motives – your decision might influence their career prospects, b) their ability to describe situations so you can actually detect your behaviour in it – fluffy generalities won't help you, and c) if you do choose to seek an expert opinion rather than an observation, then make sure it in an area where they are really qualified (it's only an expert opinion in those situations where they are experts, but we tend to extrapolate: one recent series of financial service adverts featured a presenter from a numerical game show).

2. **If you ask for it, don't get upset if you don't like it (instead, be forensic).** Francois de La Rochefoucauld said, "Few people have the wisdom to prefer the criticism that would do them good, to the praise that deceives them." The messenger might be clumsy in the way they express themselves. If you shoot them, you'll never get any more out of them (or what you do get will be disinformation designed to massage your ego and keep the messenger from taking another bullet). If the other party says something you don't want to hear ("Staff morale is poor and they think you don't take any notice of the employee survey", or "Our engineers are playing fast and loose with the safety rules because they think you prioritise profits over compliance, and the operation is an accident waiting to happen" or "Managers at two levels below you are turning a blind eye to traders' non-compliant behaviour despite repeated warnings from risk managers") you need to take a forensic approach. Get them to restate their message in sensory specific (video descriptive) terms that you can validate or safely dismiss. Make allowances for other people's clumsiness in expressing their messages.

By the way, in general, having seen messenger after messenger shot for speaking truth to power, most people keep their mouths shut, or offer sugar-coated platitudes. As events of the last decade show all too well, this leads to serious blind-spots and costs much treasure and sometimes, in safety-critical industries, blood, too. You must ensure you have ways to get the information people try to keep from you.

3. **Rather than shooting the messenger, be Machiavellian.**[8] How is the prince to deal with the conflicting needs to avoid blind-spots yet maintain the dignity required of their position? Machiavelli's prescription is elegant. You should have carefully selected advisors, and only they are allowed to give you their views. You should insist that they tell it to you straight (and ensure this through rewards and punishments as appropriate). You should also insist that they only give you advice when you ask for it. Add a good whistleblower policy (and insist that whistleblowers come up with verifiable evidence), mystery shop your own business (yourself wherever possible), and you will be well informed.

## *Giving Feedback*

The more you consciously seek your own feedback, using the approaches above, the more you will naturally get better at ensuring others get useful feedback too. Giving and receiving really are two sides of the same coin.

The key extra dimension is to recognise that most people are like Winston Churchill when he said, "I am

---

[8] I am indebted to my friend Alastair Dryburgh for drawing my attention to Machiavelli's advice on this topic.

always ready to learn something; I am not always ready to be taught."

If you show yourself to be a willing seeker of feedback for yourself, it will be easier. It's incredibly powerful if you say to one of your direct reports: "Look. More important than the feedback I give you is the feedback you get for yourself, because that way you are building your self-reliance and ability to take a lead. At the same time, it's really powerful to have outside input because we all lose sight of the wood for the trees sometimes. Here's how I go about getting feedback, and I'd like to suggest we take a similar approach."

## Seven Keys for Ensuring Good Feedback to Your People

These keys apply both in your one-to-one relationships with direct reports, and to the process of feedback within the organization as a whole.

1. **Make sure you have a learning context first.**
   Like all successful influence, the context –
   especially the shared understanding of what kind
   of relationship you are engaged in – makes all the
   difference to the meaning of and response to you
   communication. Think about a tough mentor (or
   boss, or fitness trainer, or sports coach – someone
   engaged with you in something that you really
   cared about) who you really respected, and who
   you knew to be committed to your success. You
   would take candid and even brusque input from
   them and *use it positively* even if it bruised a bit.
   Compare that with your response when you have
   no respect for the source of input. Then, even the
   most diplomatically couched message – especially
   the dreaded feedback sandwich – can be like
   crumbs in the bedclothes. What's the internal
   dialogue of most sales teams when they are
   listening to the manager giving them a pep-talk?

What's your internal dialogue like when being appraised by someone you don't respect? Not conducive to high performance, is it?

2. **Agree clear goals with recognisable evidence.** We have already discussed this process when we dealt with your own feedback requirements. Think yourself into the other person's situation and verify that they will have the information they need to be self-steering. Do your salespeople and purchasing agents know the effects of their decisions on your cash flow, for example?

3. **Ask questions to encourage active engagement in feedback seeking.** If I'm coaching a leader in the way they conduct their senior team meetings, it's far more powerful (not to say less error-prone) to say, "Did you notice how Julia responded when you changed the subject?" rather than, "You snubbed Julia by ignoring her contribution."

4. **Make feedback as specific as possible: use video description**. Remember, they can only turn your message into feedback if they can recognise their behaviour in the information coming back to them. Don't say, "That was a great presentation", say, "Because you highlighted the key figures rather than cluttering the screen with a mass of data, and then gave people the chance to ask questions of clarification before moving on, more people got involved in the subsequent discussion and gave their clear verbal agreement to the final decision, rather than the usual passive acquiescence."

5. **Focus on behaviour/skills used as well as results.** The Army has a saying: "The other side gets a vote." In business, results depend to some degree on the decisions of people outside our control (a good business design attempts to

minimise that as much as possible of course, but that external factor always exists). If you only provide binary win/lose feedback, there just isn't enough, or frequent enough, steering information for people who are learning, or are engaged in completely new endeavours. So make sure feedback shows how well people are performing the skills likely to produce success.

6. **Use the 3Q formula to build on strength.** Rather than the manipulation-prone feedback sandwich, remember the three coaching questions: What did they do that worked? What did they do better this time than last time? What do you suggest they work on next?

7. **Make feedback frequent and timely.** You know what it's like trying to have a phone call with a delay, or adjusting the shower temperature in a hotel when there's a delay? Delays make it hard for people to relate their behaviour to its results. What does that mean for the learning ability of organizations where the only 'feedback' people get is at a yearly appraisal?

## *Final Thoughts*

Understanding feedback as steering information simultaneously makes it more useful and less threatening. Disappointing results can then be reinterpreted not as evidence of final failure, but as clues as to what to do in order to improve. And successful results can be mined for insights as to what to do to build further success in the future.

Set things up at the outset with feedback in mind, then you can get and give feedback easily. It is a vital element underlying all successful performance and learning.

Of course nobody wants to hear of disappointing results, and even if you adopt the feedback mindset, it can still be a bruise to the ego. Leaders in particular must be alert to their tendency to avoid such news, as the history of the last decade makes only too clear.

Finally, remember the key to understanding and unlocking the dramatic performance-enhancing potential of feedback: in order to learn, you (and they) have to be able to recognise your actions in the results.

# CHAPTER EIGHTEEN

# DEVELOPING A RANGE OF LEADERSHIP STYLES

Rather than think about leadership as a magical, charismatic and rare quality, let's continue to look at learnable, down-to-earth ways to improve day-to-day performance. This chapter focuses on concrete actions that leaders engage in with their teams (for those interested, it's based on the work of Victor Vroom and Phillip Yetton).

Let's say you have to make a decision about the direction you and your team need to go in to respond to a particular issue. You have at least five choices:

1. Make the decision yourself – just tell the group what to do.

2. Ask for information from each person individually. Don't tell them why you need it, just get the info, then make the decision yourself and inform them of what's going to happen.

3. Ask for information from each individual, but this time, tell them why you need it, and involve them in discussing it with you. Then make the decision yourself.

4. Get the group together, and put the issue out for discussion. Listen to their ideas, question and probe etc. Let them make recommendations. Then make the decision yourself.

5. Turn the issue over to the group. Let them decide. You just back them up whatever they select.

You can think of other choices (e.g. delegating to an individual), but these five give a good range. Clearly none of these is going to be the best in all situations, and that's not the idea. Rather, the power of this comes when you consider key dimensions of the decision to be made and pick the best choice for the circumstances.

## *Matching The Style to The Situation*

To show you what I mean, here are three questions which are likely to matter in all situations:

1.  How much information do you have about the issue?

2.  How much time have you got?

3.  How much will it take to get commitment from the group?

Some examples of how this can work:

*   If you have all the information needed, have a group that are committed, and have no time, then choose Style 1.

*   If you have less information and less commitment (maybe you are new to this job and group) then you need to invest more time – Style 3 or 4 are going to make more sense.

*   If you have to maintain confidentiality, and you need more information, you can choose Style 2. You may save time, too, but at the cost fuelling rumours.

*   Maybe you don't care what the outcome of the decision is as long as there is one (e.g. venue for a staff leaving do). Then choose Style 5. It saves time and ensures commitment.

Many leaders use just one of these styles for all their decisions. Realising you have choices is liberating, and both research and experience confirm that it leads to improved results, too.

## *Further Dimensions*

There are other dimensions you can consider. For example, Styles 3 and 4 give you the opportunity to involve people in the decision process with you, thereby enabling you to coach people and develop their skills. On the other hand, if you have a trusted long-time lieutenant who is very committed and understands the way things work, you can save *both* of you a lot of time by using Style 1.

Instead of a fruitless search for the one best way (which doesn't exist), or attempting somehow to develop a magical charisma, this approach makes a difference immediately to your time use, the commitment of your people and their development. You can get into this approach in much more detail by following up on Vroom and Yetton, but the basic power of this approach is now available for you to use.

## *Final Thoughts*

I notice coaching clients and mentees often – explicitly or implicitly – trying to work out what type of leader they should be, as if there were a single consistent style that provided the answer. The lesson of this chapter is that it is often necessary to be a *flexible* type of leader. Followers differ, as do situations. It is unreasonable to expect a one-size-fits-all leadership style to work consistently.

## CONFRONTING POOR PERFORMANCE
## "THE COLUMBO WAY"

How do you confront poor performance from a staff member, supplier or subcontractor? Too often I hear about people letting unsatisfactory situations ride in the vain hope that they will get better. Others lose their temper; the resulting emotionally-charged exchanges damage the working relationship and can even end up creating legal problems.

So, a situation has arisen and you are determined that it cannot go unacknowledged. Let's assume that:

- You have observable and or documented evidence of the shortfall (i.e. it's not hearsay).
- You don't know the cause.
- You don't want to jump to conclusions (and potentially end up with egg on your face).
- You prefer not to be aggressive if at all possible.

I often recommend what I call the Columbo Technique. It avoids embarrassment if the other party has got a good reason, but it also gives them nowhere to go for excuses if they are at fault, because it focuses solely on incontrovertible evidence – things that can't be disputed.

**1. Start out by expressing puzzlement.** "Could you help me out here? There's something I don't understand."

**2. Present incontrovertible evidence:**
"Our contract says X, but what actually happened was Y."

"We agreed at the last senior team that we would all support this initiative, but your people don't seem to have made the coordination meetings."

**3. If possible, say something true and supportive that's in contrast to the problematic performance:**
"You bring us excellent stuff when you get round to it."

"You're enthusiastic once you're in the meeting."

"Your guys have really made a huge contribution to previous projects."

**4. Point out that it seems inconsistent with your legitimate expectations and request that they clear up your confusion.**
"Which is why I don't get it... is there something I'm missing that I need to know?"

You don't need a cigar and brown raincoat for this, but if you can get the spirit of Peter Falk's eye twinkle and mystified shrug, it does seem to work better!

This is a bit like the idea in Fisher and Ury's classic book on negotiation *Getting to Yes*: being soft on the person and hard on the problem. If the problem is out of character, it will often turn out that they have had a crisis for which you can make an allowance or even offer support. If they are genuinely at fault, you minimise the chances of distraction or smokescreen tactics from the other side: just keep coming back to: "It's supposed to be X, but it's Y. How come?"

However you handle it, my experience time-and-again is that the single most common cause of organizational underperformance is the tolerated under-performance or poor behaviour of a key individual. If that individual is accountable to you, you must deal with it. If you don't, then you are part of the problem.

# CHAPTER NINETEEN

# LEADING IN AMBIGUOUS AND UNSTRUCTURED SITUATIONS

*"In technical climbing, the... thing about leading
as opposed to seconding, is that when you are
seconding, the moves are as impossible for you
as they are for the lead climber, but you are
protected. As the lead climber you have to decide
how much risk you're willing to take. When you
are seconding, your lead climber is already on a
station where he or she is locked in and sitting
there so that if you fall you're going to be caught.
When you become a lead climber, suddenly
a whole new dimension to the sport occurs."*

John Grinder, co-founder of NLP
and experienced technical climber

## *Reducing Ambiguity: A Key Leadership Role*

People in junior roles usually start off working to highly
fixed procedures. In the case of many professionals –
bankers, lawyers, engineers, accountants – those
procedures may take years to master. With competence
and mastery comes promotion.

And then a rather inconvenient thing happens. The
further up the leadership ladder you get promoted, the
more you are confronted with unstructured situations
for which there is no fixed procedure. Briefs from those
you work for become less clear, multiple reporting
lines create real or apparent conflicts of priorities, and

you come face to face with the inherent (and massive) uncertainty of the wider world: the world of markets, politics, shifting trends and demographics.

A primary part of your role becomes to reduce ambiguity and to create structure for the people following you, after all, those objectives, policies, standards, regulations, strategies and plans have to come from somewhere. Just as for the new lead climber, a whole new dimension of the game opens up.

## What it Takes: Tolerance for Ambiguity

We need to accept that ambiguity and uncertainty are facts of life, the more so as your seniority increases. Some people find the challenge of that uncertainty exciting; for others it is frustrating or even frightening. Almost everyone struggles with ambiguity at times, and psychologists tell us that only a relatively small proportion of the population have a high tolerance for ambiguous situations (and some have such a low tolerance that frankly they are unlikely ever to be effective leaders).

What about the majority, the people in between? Is an ability to function well in ambiguous and unstructured situations actually something you can improve?

I believe the answer to that is *yes*, but within limits that can only be determined by trying. And if that answer irritates you, it's because you find the uncertainty it contains difficult to cope with – so read on!

## A Picture of Creative Problem Solving

Have you ever been given an unclear assignment or project brief, with a time limit for delivery, huge amounts of *potentially* relevant information, and no clear idea what a solution would look like? Think about how the following picture applies to this kind of situation:

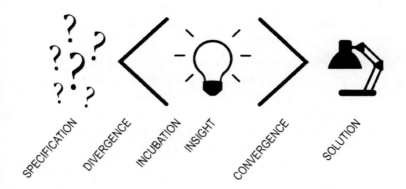

Figure 19.1: Creative problem solving

The picture was formulated by design expert JC Jones to capture the essentials of a creative design process. You start with a brief – which may be very vague – and you end up with a precise product (or document, or plan, or computer program etc.) There are four elements:

- On the right, towards the end of the process, is the "convergent" phase in which the various elements of a solution are assembled. This may be technically demanding, but it is well-defined – the ambiguity is quite low – and an expert will typically apply themselves effectively to execute the technicalities required.

- On the left, at the start of the process (labelled "divergent") is the part that drives many people crazy. What's the source of the craziness? People caught up in the divergent phase often say things such as, "I've gathered loads of information but I don't know if I have enough yet. I can't see a pattern. I am overwhelmed and swimming in data. I am working hard but making no progress. The deadline is looming but I don't know what to do...etc." They are like someone confronted with the pieces of a large jigsaw scattered across the living room floor.

- In the middle of the diagram is a light bulb. This represents the "Aha!" moment when you see the lid on the jigsaw box. At that point, a pattern emerges out of all the confusing data, and while you still have the work of convergent thinking, you can see where you are going.

- Preceding the light bulb is a period (of unknown length!) called "incubation". The transition from a sea of unrelated information to the flash of insight often comes only after you have slept on a question for a while, or while you are doing something else (Archimedes had his Eureka moment when he was relaxing in the bath).

I once showed this to a team of corporate graphic designers. They very much recognised the pattern, and then one of them said: "That explains in a nutshell why my job is so stressful; for me, the Eureka moment has a deadline!" This is undoubtedly one of the biggest challenges to the disciplined middle-level manager who is promoted to the next level: you can't accurately plan or allocate time for incubation.

## Understand Your Need for Closure

As a hundred military misadventures, thousands of failed software projects and millions of poorly constructed business presentations confirm, there is a huge problem with rushing from a vague specification to immediate convergence on a solution.

People rush the process because they need psychological closure – divergence creates tension, and many people will do anything to reduce that tension as soon as possible.

The danger is that if you can't tolerate ambiguity you will adopt a bad course of action just to release the tension. And worse, some people will build an elaborate case for saying that no action is necessary when it manifestly is – again to feel that they have the situation nicely boxed up. British industry has often done this – think about the complacency over the Japanese car and motorcycle industries, or contemporary denial in the face of the Chinese and Indian entrepreneurship and innovation increasingly reported in the business media.

## Seven Keys for Handling Ambiguity and Uncertainty

These keys have proven themselves effective as general prescriptions and they are a great place to start. Recognise too that you may find certain aspects of the challenge easier or more difficult to deal with depending on your own individual psychology. Use these as a reliable starting point, and if necessary, engage the help of a mentor, coach or other trusted advisor to deal with any further specific issues.

### Faced with an ambiguous situation, locate your progress on the divergence-convergence map and recognise your need for closure

Earlier I mentioned how the graphic designer got a flash of recognition in response to the divergence-convergence picture. Once you understand the dynamic, you can use it to help you navigate. Just knowing that a lack of closure is normal, or even desirable, at this phase in the process will in itself help to reduce feelings of uncertainty. It will also prevent you from unknowingly rushing too quickly to an ill-thought-out solution.

## Accept that it may be that *you* have to define the situation

This point is not about skills or personality traits; it's about giving yourself permission to lead. If you have spent years learning diligently to deliver to other people's precise specifications, and in accordance with their tightly defined procedures, an active shift of mind is required. As a leader you have to be clear: defining the situation is up to you. This is one of those times where you have to "step up".

## Get clear on your purpose

The best response to the question, "I don't know what to do" is usually, "Well what are you *really* trying to achieve?" As obvious as this is, it's amazing how often people seem to forget it. NASA spent a fortune on developing a pen that would write in weightless conditions – the Russians gave their cosmonauts pencils. Who was clearer on their purpose?

The purpose hierarchy in Figure 19.2 is a useful way to make sure you will select actions that achieve your real purposes.

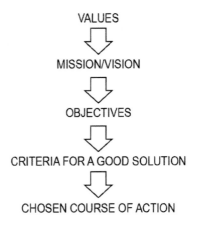

VALUES

MISSION/VISION

OBJECTIVES

CRITERIA FOR A GOOD SOLUTION

CHOSEN COURSE OF ACTION

Figure 19.2: The purpose hierarchy

Here's how you use it. Say you are given a vague brief such as, "Improve cross-functional collaboration".

If you start by "brainstorming" a load of possible courses of action, you will likely end up either with a poor solution or a huge range from which you are unable to chose.

If, however, you stop and take a little time to focus toward the top of the hierarchy, you will ask better questions, for example:

- What values are we trying to promote by improving cross-functional collaboration? What is the fit with our mission/purpose?
- What objectives, if achieved, would represent fulfilment of those intentions?
- What would a good solution look like (in terms of e.g. resources used, risks, cultural fit, ease of implementation)
- What alternatives might meet those criteria?
- And only then, which is the most preferred option?

If this seems almost like a mini strategy process, you are right. A strategist seeks a balance between overall aims, external opportunities or threats, and internal resources. Doing so requires a high tolerance of divergence and ambiguity. It is also the stuff of leadership.

### Actively seek comments and feedback on "draft" plans and assumptions

In order to lead, you need people to follow. A consultant I know does strategy work with law firms. Law firms are generally partnerships and the process of managing them has been likened to that of herding cats. And of course lawyers are professionally trained to find loopholes and problems with proposals. So this consultant's challenge is to help define a situation and a solution without being shot down and losing the credibility required to maintain influence. One of his tricks is that "every document is a draft". People asked for an opinion on a draft are generally far more helpful and charitable than those asked to consider a final version.

If you are seeking verbal input from stakeholders, here is a magic phrase for getting time and comment from people who can help you: "Can I run something by you quickly?" Try it and you will find it creates a constructive dynamic even with people you may find difficult to approach (e.g. very senior busy executives, political rivals).

## Start projects early and build in incubation time

Any lecturer will tell you that even though they set coursework assignments ten weeks before the deadline, many people still submit late. You may think this is laziness, and sometimes it is. Many times, however, conscientious students start a bit late because they fear the difficulty of the task, and then get caught in a dilemma between endless divergence (hunting for more and more material in the library) and abortive attempts at ill-defined convergence (an essay that just won't come together). In my lecturing days, I always advised students to at least consider the assignment as early in the term as possible, so that they were mulling it over (incubating it) "on the mental back-burner".

Most ignored me of course, but those who adopted the advice found it worked, and this was usually reflected in their (blind-marked!) results.

## Realise that there is usually more than one way to skin a cat

Much professional education reinforces an assumption that there is one best solution for problems, and that the job demands that you must find and implement it. Not to do so is to be "wrong", which is "very bad". This is generally true within technical disciplines, but in business more widely, where we lack perfect information and where time is money, "good enough" now is usually better than "perfect" later. Effective leaders know when they are in a situation where there are multiple ways to get an acceptable result, and they don't agonise over the choice among those ways.

## Accept that there is no return without some risk

What if you act without perfect knowledge and it doesn't work out? Well, then you, like all leaders do from time to time, will fall short. Will that matter? Honestly, it depends on the prevalent culture. In the US, one or two failures are almost expected of an entrepreneur in order for them to be taken seriously. In the UK, backers may be less charitable. In some military organizations, where being proactive is vital and standing about can be fatal, there is a stated policy of rewarding even failed attempts at initiative while punishing passivity.

What if you are promoted in a culture which then punishes attempts to take initiative? Well then you have three choices: give up and conform (not really leadership), leave and find something more conducive (perfectly valid), or decide to change the culture (risky but, of course, the stuff of real leaders).

## *Final Thoughts*

The inability to respond effectively to ambiguous situations is probably the most commonly mentioned issue I hear from senior executives about their direct reports.

Someone has to be the lead climber, or else no one will get to make the ascent. Building an organization, creating wealth, providing jobs and fulfilling work, delivering products and services to make life more comfortable – all these things depend on those who is prepared to enter into uncertain and ambiguous situations and give them shape.

The majority of people are of course not prepared to do this. Therein lies the opportunity for those who are, or who are prepared to develop themselves to overcome their discomfort with ambiguity and pursue the rewards of leadership.

## HAVE WE OVER-PROMOTED THIS PERSON?

This issue is a frequent trigger of requests for coaching. Someone is promoted because they do an excellent job at one level, but their performance at the next is judged inadequate. Here are five key aspects to consider if you suspect over-promotion. It's really important to consider the first two in order.

**1. This first key can save a lot of trouble. What's the *evidence* for under-performance?**
Have you observed it yourself? If all you have so far is stories, are you being set up? Maybe this person is actually competent, but they are being used as an easy target by *other* people with other agendas. You've got to exclude such possibilities first. For example, at one client a new business manager had been promoted from the ranks. Others were jealous of their progress. The "evidence" of incompetence was actually a series of malicious reports from former peers.

**2. Is there some personal issue that has coincided with the promotion – i.e. it's not the new job, it's something else.**
Use the Columbo Technique on page 194.

Assuming you have been able to eliminate these possibilities...

**3. How are the job demands different from what they were doing before? Is it even the same *kind* of job anymore?**
There are a number of such transitions to be made on the way up through any substantial organization. One classic example is the salesperson to sales manager transition, another is the transition from functional to general manager. Are the differences around skills, priorities or time use? Political ability? Financial acumen? Big-picture perspective? Sheer stamina?

**4. Is the motivation really there?**

What people will often admit to a coach, but not to their manager, is they were flattered at the promotion, their spouse is pleased, they need the money and status, but they'd rather not have the extra accountability that goes with a senior line position (but then they don't get those rewards). Would they be better in a professional support or a "super sales star" role?

**5. Can they acquire the capacities required to handle new role demands, and is it worthwhile to attempt to do so?**

If they really want those rewards, then skills can be learned. Sometimes, however, the skills can be addressed, just not for a realistic investment. Slow learners may get there in the end, but the price may be too high (for the organization or the individual).

There's a fine line between a stretch assignment and over-promotion. These five keys are a good place to start if there is any doubt. If it does turn out to be over-promotion, it's usually possible to engineer a dignified move into a more comfortable role, and failing that (in hopefully rarer cases), to get acceptance that it's time for them to "consider their future with the organization elsewhere". In most cases an excellent outcome can be reached, and with the right support through the transition, the person goes on to thrive.

CONCLUSION

# Strategic Leadership, Organizational Culture and the Three Stories

The progress of your business depends on decisions. But not just your own. It bears repeating that success crucially depends on multiple, sometimes repeated decisions taken by your:

- **Customers/Clients** (Give you a try this time instead of my usual supplier? Give you an order? Give you another order?)

- **Talent** (Apply? Accept an offer of employment? Accept pay and conditions? Follow safety procedures? Go the extra mile for a customer or cut a corner and save time and effort?)

- **Backers** (Fund this project? Buy stock? Extend credit? Provide access to distribution? Provide more time? Roll over the debt? Pull the plug?)

These decisions are the moments of truth that shape the nature and direction of your business and therefore determine its ultimate survival and prosperity. This is where strategy meets execution, or implementation, every day, and your success as a leader depends on your ability to influence all these decisions!

First you have to know what you want each of these people to decide, and secondly you have to maximise your chances that they will decide your way. So what makes the three stories compelling?

# *Eight Keys to Punching Through With Your Stories*

Here are eight keys to transmitting your message and having it influence moments of truth:

## 1. Understand the 'motivation structure' of each stakeholder

Each of your audiences has a different motivation structure. In a nutshell, they value different things, and they want to avoid different things. The key to influencing them is to present your story so that it demonstrates that deciding your way moves them *away from* what they want to avoid, and *towards* what they want to gain.

Figure 20.1 provides a questioning framework which you can use to understand the motivation structure of someone you are trying to reach. Sometimes you can question them directly, and other times – especially when dealing with large groups – you will have to gain the information by other routes (probably some combination of interviews, focus groups and direct observation of behaviour and/or data).

However you get the information, if you can put yourself in their shoes and answer these questions, you will be well on the way to creating a compelling story.

Once you have their motivation structure mapped out, the point is to appeal to the things they care about rather than the things you care about. For example (this one is hard for the types of people who become senior executives to grasp), your employees often care a hell of a lot more about their relationship with their immediate supervisor and the perceived relative fairness of their pay than they do about their absolute pay level or your company's ROCE. But what do most executives talk about to staff?

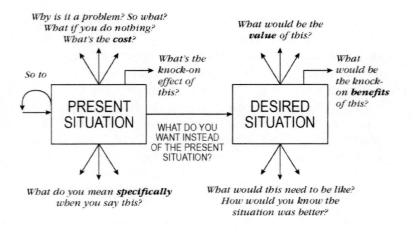

Figure 20.1: A guide to understanding
your audience's motivation structure

Your B2B customer – for all their talk to the contrary – may care much more about their own bonus and promotion than they do about the technical superiority of your offering vis-á-vis an entrenched, blue-chip, competitor. Ideally of course, the two sets of interests will coincide, but they very often do not, especially in large matrix organizations.

Your story will be much more compelling it if refers to their motivations, at least implicitly. A corny but accurate old-time sales adage actually holds up well here: "If you see John Brown through John Brown's eyes, you'll sell John Brown what John Brown buys."

## 2. Put your stories in *the receiver's* terms

One newly-appointed CEO I know told his private equity backers – very reasonably and logically – that it was too early after his first six months to have settled on a well-formed strategy. There was too much uncertainty and too many possible avenues which he and his senior team had still to evaluate, and therefore he wasn't prepared to make major resource allocation decisions.

The backer was very unhappy with what he perceived as vagueness. So the next month, the CEO reformulated his message and said, "We are going to engage in a series of strategic 'controlled experiments' to understand the fast-changing market and determine which ideas are the most promising". The backer was delighted.

A manager I know realised that his graduate recruits were unmoved by the company's new share plan – they just didn't get it. Until, that is, he explained that it amounted to "free money". That got their attention and they then became interested enough to understand it in more orthodox terms.

### 3. Remember that business logic and personal emotion must support each other

Your graduate recruits might indeed stand to gain hugely from your new share plan or enhanced benefit package, but have you noticed how many of them don't get excited about it as much as they do about a much smaller present-value pay-rise? As with your backers, you have to make the future value compelling *now*.

The hard-bitten procurement professional who is acting for your customer wants to get the cheapest price for a personal reason: because they think that demonstrates that they are competent to their peers ("Boy, did I extract a deal from them!"), and may do that even at the expense of lost quality or poorer working capital management.

### 4. Don't oversell

Once people have got excited, they will want to check your logic. Or at least, they will expect that things do indeed happen as you have promised.

## 5. Make facts and data "live"

Choose your media and examples to make the "what ifs" of the situation real to the listener. For example, if I tell the story of the Bay of Pigs fiasco (see Chapter Fourteen) to a board of directors, I am implicitly showing them that stifling debate, or lacking the courage to speak up, lead to disaster. If I follow that up with a discussion of the Challenger disaster and then talk about corporate manslaughter legislation, I am going to make an increasingly strong impression.

Similarly, if you tell your employees about secretaries at GE or Microsoft who retired wealthy because of stock options they took up earlier in their careers, you will encourage enthusiasm for your share plan far more dramatically than you will by bombarding them with bullet points about the terms of the scheme.

## 6. Don't assume the receiver shares your context

I go to more than my fair share of quarterly corporate presentations to staff. Invariably there is a slide with financial results on it, perhaps reporting the company's return on capital or some other performance ratio. While this information is both salient and interesting to the person who understands it, the fact is that many people who work for you don't understand it! When the executive droning through the PowerPoint slides reaches this item, I like to look at the audience and try to work out how many of them have a grasp of the terminology, or the significance of the metrics being quoted. When I've had a chance to ask discreetly afterwards, many admit that they have no clue. The only message staff take from such a presentation is "this is not for me".

## 7. Believe it

In my experience, people in most organizations, regardless of size or sector, are on a hair-trigger when it comes to cynicism about "stuff management says". They have been reinforced in this orientation not only by their experiences at work, but by the constant games between politicians and journalists that they see and hear in the media, and of course by the simple knowledge, acquired early in life, that there can be advantages to saying things you don't mean.

We've all heard CEOs say "People are our greatest resource"; a fine sentiment, even if expressed in clichéd words. But often the statement carries zero credibility with the staff, because the company's actions contradict it.

How many times has your company launched an initiative with a name like "Breakthrough 2015" (pick your own date), only to forget about it, or supersede it with another initiative before the first one has come to fruition? The more you do this, the less they believe you.

The solution is to believe what you say, and say what you believe. Not to do so over an extended period can quite simply ruin an organization, and stymie any leader's ability to get meaningful progress achieved through their people.

## 8. It's about "quality of earnings"

At the risk of being abstract, I believe leaders of businesses both large and small need a "philosophy of business". They definitely don't have to be able to give a dissertation on it, but they do have to transmit it – in fact can't help but transmit it – in their everyday words and actions to the stakeholders who hold the key to success.

You can make money by neglecting one or more of your audiences in the short term, or by saying one thing while meaning another, but ultimately leadership is also about "quality of earnings" – what kind of business, organization and market are you leading towards?

## *Final Thoughts*

A leader's day job is to get things done through other people. It's easy to assume that this just means giving instructions to people within your direct, formal reporting structure, but that isn't even a good definition of simple 'managing'.

Leadership is about taking the initiative, going first, being proactive, and building relationships in order to get things done – in new ways if necessary. Of course that takes place within agreed boundaries (legal, financial, policy, values etc.), but within those boundaries, it's a lot more than simply managing to set procedures. It requires a degree of courage, flexibility of approach and a commitment not merely to tasks, but to *results*.

Taking a step back, notice how much of leading is about influencing perceptions and interpreting events so that people understand that it is in their best interests to follow your desired course of action.

And that brings us back to the three stories. Learn to formulate and articulate compelling stories to customers, investors and talented people! There is probably no higher-yielding personal development objective for ambitious leaders.

*Conclusion*

# About the Author

Andrew is the founder and principal of BassClusker Consulting, a firm which helps leaders to make existing resources and relationships more productive through provocative thinking. Andrew has the ability to cut through jargon and buzzwords, translating solid theory into practical steps which make a real difference to clients. He has worked across a wide range of industries and sectors including professional services, banking, automotive, insurance and health, in the UK, Europe and CIS.

Andrew has a PhD in Software Engineering and a BSc in Computer Science and Applied Psychology from Aston University. Prior to co-founding BassClusker, Andrew lectured at Aston Business School, where he was director of the Psychology and Management programme. When not engaged in his own client work, he continues to contribute to the school's Master's and Executive Development programmes.

An active member of the Birmingham (UK) business community, Andrew is a Board Director of the professional services lobbying and networking group Birmingham Forward, and acts as advisor to the Birmingham Future Mentoring Scheme.

Outside of work, Andrew plays lead guitar in a tribute band dedicated to the music of Canadian progressive rock band Rush, and dabbles in the dangerous world of stand-up comedy (with decidedly mixed results!)

For further resources, visit: www.bassclusker.com